STUDENT VOICE

100 Argument Essays by Teens on Issues That Matter to Them

Norton Books in Education

STUDENT VOICE

100 Argument Essays by Teens on Issues That Matter to Them

An Anthology from
The New York Times
Learning Network

KATHERINE SCHULTEN

W. W. NORTON & COMPANY
Independent Publishers Since 1923

Note to Readers: Essays in this volume were selected from among the winners and runners-up in Student Editorial Contests administered between 2014 and 2019 by The New York Times Learning Network. In very limited instances, modifications have been made for consistency with the publisher's policies and house style, or to reflect the passage of time.

Cover art by Sydney A. Christiansen, who was 16 years old
when she created it for The New York Times Learning Network in 2018.

Printed in the United States of America
First Edition

For information about permission to reproduce selections from this book, write to Permissions, W. W. Norton & Company, Inc., 500 Fifth Avenue, New York, NY 10110

For information about special discounts for bulk purchases, please contact W. W. Norton Special Sales at specialsales@wwnorton.com or 800-233-4830

Manufacturing by LSC Harrisonburg
Book design by Vicki Fischman
Production manager: Katelyn MacKenzie

Library of Congress Cataloging-in-Publication Data

Names: Schulten, Katherine, editor.
Title: Student voice : 100 argument essays by teens on issues that matter to them / [edited by] Katherine Schulten.
Description: First edition. | New York : W.W. Norton & Company, 2020. | Series: Norton books in education | Includes bibliographical references and index.
Identifiers: LCCN 2020023294 | ISBN 9780393714302 (paperback) | ISBN 9780393714319 (epub)
Subjects: LCSH: Teenagers' writings, American. | American essays—21st century.
Classification: LCC PS683.T45 S78 2020 | DDC 814/.60809283—dc23
LC record available at https://lccn.loc.gov/2020023294

W. W. Norton & Company, Inc., 500 Fifth Avenue, New York, N.Y. 10110
www.wwnorton.com

W. W. Norton & Company Ltd., 15 Carlisle Street, London W1D 3BS

4 5 6 7 8 9 0

For my mother, who taught me that the best afternoons are spent on the couch with a book.

And for my students at Edward R. Murrow High School, who gave me the ten happiest years of my career.

Contents

Acknowledgments

This book would not exist if Michael Gonchar, my fellow Learning Network editor, hadn't come up with the idea for running a student editorial contest in the first place. It was his vision for how the contest could work that has made it a hit with teachers since 2014. Over the years we have switched roles—first I was his boss, and now he is mine—but regardless of our titles, thinking about The Learning Network together has always been a wonderful, creative collaboration. Thank you, Michael, for being the best work partner I can imagine.

Student Voice would also not exist if Jane Bornemeier, editor of New York Times Special Sections, hadn't agreed to run some of these essays in print in 2018, where Norton education editor Carol Collins first read them and suggested to us they become a book. Thank you, Jane, for partnering with The Learning Network to spotlight the work of teens and teachers, and thank you to Special Sections deputy editor Jill Agostino and art director Corinne Myller for making it so fun and rewarding to create those pages together.

Carol Collins didn't just spot the potential for this book, she also guided it from start to finish. Carol, thank you for your brilliance in shaping what began as a fairly unwieldy project, and for your thoughtfulness about every tiny step along the way. I'm grateful to the entire team at W. W. Norton for believing in *Student Voice* and making it and *Raising Student Voice*, the Teacher's Companion, work so well together. Thank you to Mariah Eppes, who so ably shepherded it through multiple drafts, to Laura Goldin, for her expert legal counsel, to Katelyn MacKenzie, who managed the book's production, to Anna Reich, who facilitated the cover design, to Irene Vartanoff, for her excellent copyediting, and Jamie Vincent, who assisted with permissions and all of the other logistical details.

I also owe a debt to several more people at The New York Times, especially Alex Ward, who was Editorial Director of Book Development when Carol proposed the idea, and whose kindness and entertaining knowledge of Times book-history helped me believe I could do this. Thank you also to Nicholas Kristof, who has always generously said yes to Learning Network invitations, and whose golden advice on opinion-writing is woven throughout the Teacher's Companion. Thank you to Peter Catapano, Caroline Que, Brian Rideout, and Lee Riffaterre who helped smooth the way for these books, and met my nervous questions and concerns with expert guidance. And thank you to The Times itself, both for inventing The Learning Network in 1998 and for continuing to support it despite the many rocky years for the news industry since.

But most of all, thank you to the students and teachers who come to our site each spring and take part in our Student Editorial Contest. As a former teacher (and student!) myself, I know how much work went into every piece here, as well as into the thousands of others we receive annually. It is an honor and a joy to be an audience for them.

Finally, thank you to my family. To my parents, Carey and Judith Schulten, who set the best example possible for how to be in this world. To my children, Nick and Madeline Dulchin, who I'd rather hang around with than anyone. And, especially, to my husband, Mike Dulchin, who is the luckiest thing to have happened to me in a very lucky life.

Introduction

What makes you mad?

What do you wish more people understood?

What would you like to see change?

The essays in this book offer 100 different answers to those questions, in the voices of 100 teenagers from around the world.

Some are heartbreaking and some are funny. Some ground their arguments in personal experience while others quote facts and statistics. Some take on issues you might expect, like gun violence and the environment, college admissions and #MeToo, while others raise topics you may never have considered, from bullying in gym class to the blessings of selfie culture.

No matter what they focus on, however, they all make us care. That's one of our chief criteria for choosing winners in our annual New York Times Learning Network Student Editorial Contest each spring, and the essays in this book were selected from over 43,000 that have been submitted over the years.

The contest challenges teenagers to write about any issue they like and, in no more than 450 words, make a compelling case. We judges—Learning Network staff, volunteers from the Times Opinion section, and educators from around the country—choose the pieces that do that best, then publish them online and, often, in print as well. We look for writing that gets our attention, introduces new ideas, engages us with voice and story, and convincingly backs its claims with rich and reliable evidence.

So if you are a student whose only association with the phrase "persuasive essay" is the formulaic writing you may have learned for standardized tests, these pieces can show you that there's more to the genre. If you assume this kind of essay always has to follow a set of ironclad rules—say, that you should never use the word "I," or that it must be five paragraphs long, or that the thesis has to come at the end of the first paragraph—this book can offer you lessons in how, why, and when such "rules" might be broken, at least if your purpose is to interest a real audience.

In collecting these winning essays all in one place, we hope to offer you a set of "mentor texts" by kids your own age. Thanks to the work of people like Malala Yousafzai, Greta Thunberg, and the Parkland students, the concept of "student voice" is having a bit of a moment. Yet, as one student I interviewed pointed out, the opinion writing you study in school is still invariably by adults—"by, like, 50-year-old white guys who have been doing this for their whole careers," as he put it. This book offers you the option of learning from fellow 13–18-year-olds too, and placing their voices and concerns alongside those of professionals.

None of these essays is perfect, of course, but all of them have lessons to teach and "craft moves" you can borrow. Maybe you'll start your piece with dialogue, the way Candice C. and Cheryl B. do in **#27**, or maybe you'll end it with a final line so powerful that it deserves its own paragraph, like that in **#17** by Daina Kalnina. Perhaps Narain Dubey's essay (**#92**) will show you how to write about a tragic personal experience and make a universal point. Or maybe Sarah Celestin's piece (**#82**) will convince you that good opinion writing doesn't always have to take on profound global issues, but can sometimes just be about pizza.

As you read you'll come to see that most of these essays grew out of students' real-life interests and concerns, and they may be interests and concerns you share. For instance, like Asaka Park (**#3**) and Marco Alvarez (**#58**), you might be tired of stereotypes about a community you're part of. Or, like Tony Xiao (**#84**), you might be a gamer—or a gun owner like Paige D. (**#39**), a football player like Keegan Lindell (**#85**), have a chronic health condition like Eva Ferguson (**#68**), or firsthand experience with a broken immigration system like Safa Saleh and Kevin Morales (**#40** and **#45**). Or maybe you're just messy, like Isabel Hwang (**#9**), or sick of being last in line at school every day because, like Stephanie Zhang, your surname starts with Z (**#19**). These writers have authority on these topics because they've lived them, and they know things about them that others don't. You have that kind of authority on the issues you know firsthand, too.

So read this book to identify what others have done that you admire—and, perhaps, to find places where the work could be stronger. Listen to the way different voices emerge in the essays, even though they're only 450 words each. Notice how these writers weave in evidence of many kinds, how they vary fact and opinion, and how they support claims from "We need to take video-game addiction seriously" (**#87**) to "We should all eat more bugs" (**#78**).

Most important, read this book to figure out what you might want to say and how you might want to say it. What perspectives are missing? What could you add? Or to return to the questions we started with, What makes you mad? What do you wish more people understood? What would you like to see change?

And whether you send your writing to us or get it out into the world some other way, know this: your voice and point of view are unique, and you have opinions to express that no one else could ever write about in exactly the same way.

—Katherine Schulten, Editor,
The New York Times Learning Network

More About The Essays and The New York Times Learning Network

The 100 essays in this collection were either winners or runners up in one of The Learning Network's Student Editorial Contests between 2014 and 2019 and were chosen from among many to represent a variety of evergreen issues. As this book went into production, however, we decided to add three essays from the 2020 contest so readers could see a range of teenage responses to the coronavirus pandemic. You can find those, and more detail about them, in Appendix B. If you would like to participate, we run the contest annually in February, and you can find the rubric and rules at the back of this book, as well as online at nytimes.com/learning. Nowhere online, however, can you find this full collection, nor the material in the related Teacher's Companion.

In case you're not familiar with The New York Times Learning Network, it has been part of NYTimes.com since 1998 and has had the same mission for over 20 years—to help people teach and learn with *Times* content and thereby "bring the world into the classroom."

Over time, however, our focus has changed significantly. In 1998 The New York Times Learning Network was chiefly a place for teachers to get lesson plans. Today it is better known as a hub for student commentary on everything from politics to pop culture. We hear from nearly 1,500 teenagers a week as they post thoughts to our daily writing prompts and to our weekly discussions about *Times* photos, films, and graphics. We also run nine annual contests in addition to our Editorial Contest and invite students to create videos, political cartoons, poems, reviews, photo essays, podcasts, and more. We'd be delighted to have you join us.

Finally, a few notes on some inconsistencies you'll find in this collection:

- In 2014 and 2015, The Learning Network did not post student last names or ages unless a parent or guardian contacted us to ask that we add them. Some of the pieces from those years, then, are missing that information.
- Though these essays have been very lightly copyedited to fix obvious typos, they otherwise appear exactly as the students originally submitted them. You'll therefore find differences in style ranging from how sources are cited to whether numbers are spelled out or written as numerals.
- Our contest rules state that students need to use at least one New York Times source and at least one non-New York Times source. Many students listed only those, but some included several more. You can find those sources after each essay.

Index to the Essays

TEENAGE LIFE ONLINE

TEENAGE LIFE OFFLINE

SCHOOL

GENDER AND SEXUALITY

RACE AND RELIGION

SCIENCE, TECHNOLOGY, AND THE ENVIRONMENT

PHYSICAL AND MENTAL HEALTH

ARTS, CULTURE, AND FOOD

SPORTS AND GAMING

CRIMINAL JUSTICE AND POLICING

THE ESSAYS

Teenage Life Online

“We get to experience the world from everyone’s point of view; we’re not limited by the danger of a single story.”

“I deleted my social media because of the obsessions that overtook me.”

“Like a scene from a dystopian horror film, everywhere I turned, there was another camera out, snapping a photo.”

1 A Generation Zer's Take on the Social Media Age

by Elena Quartararo, 17 (2018)

Adults seem to think the internet is nothing more than a breeding ground for unproductivity and detachment from the "real world," that social media offers only a platform for cyberbullies and child predators. They mock us for our so-called "addiction," calling us a self-involved, attention-starved generation. But if you ask any intelligent young person—two adjectives that are not mutually exclusive—they'll tell you all about what the information superhighway really means to us.

Today's youth have come of age in an atmosphere where encroaching problems of climate change, global terrorism, economic crises and mass shootings—to name a few—have opened our eyes to the reality we're living in, the weight of fixing it all resting on our shoulders. But we've also grown up in a world where we can type into Google anything we want to learn more about; we can engage with millions of people from all walks of life, come to understand perspectives at every angle. Knowledge is powerful, and we have all that we could want available at our fingertips.

The reality is I follow news pages on my Instagram. I can't go a day on Twitter without seeing profound statements concerning the political climate. I have discussions with people over gun control and women's rights based on what I've posted on my Snapchat story. Like it or not, social media has given us a way not only to speak out, but to educate ourselves and expand our minds in a way that is unprecedented.

We've become the most tolerant and conscious generation to date, with 76 percent of Gen Zers concerned about humanity's influence on the Earth and 60 percent hoping the job they choose impacts the world. Race, religion, sexuality, gender identity and anything differing from what has so long been deemed normal are all topics we don't write off, with a revolutionary 37 percent and 21 percent not identifying as 100 percent straight or 100 percent one gender, respectively.

We get to experience the world from everyone's point of view; we're not limited by the danger of the single story, aren't held back by our own ignorance.

So, I urge adults to back off, to encourage young people to use the internet to their advantage. Because while it's easy to understand the mental and emotional drawbacks that can be associated with the cyberworld, this connection to a diverse plethora of information has given us the opportunity to reach our own conclusions about the world, to make our beliefs known, to mobilize in efforts and take a stand—from protests and marches planned by students, to educating others on registering to vote—and it has created a socially and politically aware, opinionated and unafraid youth, who are wholly prepared to change the world.

Sources

Abramovich, Giselle. "15 Mind-Blowing Stats About Generation Z." CMO.com by Adobe: Digital Marketing Insights, Expertise and Inspiration–for and by Marketing Leaders, 12 June 2015.

Barr, Caelainn. "Who Are Generation Z? The Latest Data on Today's Teens." The Guardian, 10 Dec. 2016.

Kemper, Nychele. "The March For Our Lives Was Influenced by Literature and Social Media." The Odyssey Online, 3 Apr. 2018.

Potarazu, Sreedhar. "Is Social Media Ruining Our Kids?" CNN, 22 Oct. 2015.

Williams, Alex. "Move Over, Millennials, Here Comes Generation Z." The New York Times, 18 Sept. 2015.

2 The Resurrection of Gilgamesh

by Annie Cohen, 18 (2018)

"If you don't post it, did it really happen?" These words were spoken to me, however satirical in intent, while I was sitting with 50 other teenagers at a cast party after a production of "Grease." Every single teenager present was on the phone, myself included. What else could I do? There was nobody to talk to. I was alone in a sea of phone screens. Although I chose to delete my social media many months ago, I still have not escaped its influence.

My generation has a Gilgamesh Complex, and it is enabled. Gilgamesh, for those unfamiliar, went on a quest for immortality, and when he discovered the impossibility of this act, vowed to make his name live on forever, the closest thing to immortality we humans have. Gilgamesh succeeded, as every high schooler who has read his epic knows. The problem is that fame, however short-lived, is in the grasp of every young human who has access to the Internet, American Dream Style. Everybody must have his or her name known, everybody must know who is doing what, to feed our Gilgamesh Complex.

As Karen Rosenberg said in the New York Times essay "Everyone's Lives, in Pictures," "The act of snapping a picture is no longer enough to confirm reality and enhance experience; only sharing can give us that validation." In an age in which technology reigns, people feel the need to post every meal, every party and every coffee date, to prove that it happened. Susan Sontag, quoted in Rosenberg's article, agrees with this view, saying, "Needing to have reality confirmed and experience enhanced by photographs is an aesthetic consumerism to which everyone is now addicted."

The truth of this is proved through social media use in teenagers especially. Nobody is safe from the constant blue-lighted faces of teens, but not everybody understands the inherent addiction of proving you have a life. Teenagers are known for having stages of lower self-esteem and needing confirmation for confidence. Social media provides those confirmations with simple numbers. How many people like this and how many followers you have. It is the most straightforward way to see your status.

In The Huffington Post's article "Inside the Mind of a Teen's Instagram Post," by Lauren Galley, Galley understands that teens use social media "to boost their self-esteem and gain popularity." This confirmation becomes addictive, quickly. Galley discusses how teens use social media to define their self-worth. This is unhealthy behavior, as I, as a teen, know first-hand. I deleted my social media because of the obsessions that overtook me. We are faced with a generation of people who will not all decide to delete these enablers.

Welcome back, Gilgamesh.

Sources

Galley, Lauren. "Inside the Mind of a Teen's Instagram Post." The Huffington Post. 21 Mar. 2015.

Rosenberg, Karen. "Everyone's Lives, in Pictures." The New York Times. 21 Apr. 2012.

3 I'm a Disabled Teenager, and Social Media Is My Lifeline

by Asaka Park, 17 (2019)

I'm keenly attuned to the unwritten rules of social interaction. I can identify the subtle variations in people's facial expressions, and I'm quick to read between the lines. And my discernment is not just on an intellectual level, but also at an intuitive level: I'm intimately familiar with the dance of social interaction.

The information that I just provided sounds like a mundanity, until I tell you I was diagnosed with autism. I defy the stereotypes of someone who can't possibly "get it" socially.

No one knows that I can. I can "get it."

Of course, people don't see that. I struggle with impulsivity. My physical clumsiness makes it hard for me to maintain appropriate facial expressions and tone of voice. While I easily grasp abstract concepts, I often can't convert them into tangible, step-by-step actions, making it difficult to communicate gracefully. Even the untrained eye notices these challenges, and they confound my social faux pas as a failure to understand or share other people's expectations.

I'm depleted. Every day at school, I isolate myself from most of my peers: it's a matter of time before they make these assumptions, before they postulate how my brain works. On social media, though, I'm a completely different person. I'm dynamic. I'm assertive. I'm people-oriented.

Many claim that social media distracts teens from meaningful, genuine interactions. My experiences, however, are the total opposite of that. Cultivating my own space on the Internet helped me thrive outside the pigeonhole. Namely, I use my blog to explain the real reason why I act the way I do. Even though not everyone will understand, I know some people will, and it gives me tremendous hope.

I know I'm not the only one. For many disabled people, social media gives them access to a social life and community involvement in an otherwise inaccessible world[1]. Not only does social media give me the platform to correct assumptions, people don't assume things about me in the first place, because it's a level playing field. For example, when I Tweet, my addled movements are replaced by various emojis and reaction GIFs, which gives me a vaster palette to express myself.

Furthermore, I've learned to extend the conversation on disability from my own personal circumstances to the broader issue of ableism. Don Tapscott, a media consultant, remarked, "[Teens] didn't grow up being the passive recipients of somebody else's broadcast."[2] This definitely resonated with me. I used to feel alone, not seeing girls like me on the magazine covers, but not anymore. In a click, I can create my own media where people with disabilities are seen and heard, rather than pliantly consuming the media that routinely devalue people with disabilities.

Sources

Ryan, Frances. "The Missing Link: Why Disabled People Can't Afford to #DeleteFacebook." The Guardian, Guardian News and Media, 4 April 2018.

Parker-Pope, Tara. "Are Today's Teenagers Smarter and Better Than We Think?" The New York Times, 30 March 2018.

4 Through the Cell Phone Camera Lens

by Lauren N., 16 (2016)

I walked into the obscure, dimly lit room at the hipster affiliated "Think Tank Gallery" in Downtown Los Angeles. I was amazed by the fascinating concepts and social statements made through different mediums. My eyes darted around the room, internalizing all of the work, and figuring out which piece to analyze next. The group of women I was with, however, seemed to look at the art through different lenses: the camera lenses on their cell phones.

The gallery was like a scene from a dystopian horror film, plagued by cell phones, opened Snapchats and Instagram photos. Instead of walking freely through the gallery, I had to stop every five feet so that I didn't get in someone's picture. It was like dodging bullets in some high speed action adventure. Everywhere I turned, there was another camera out, snapping a photo for social media.

Ironically, the gallery was called "Think Tank," possibly because the creators wanted to provoke ideas from the viewer. Instead, there was only the absence of thought in that big, cellphone littered room. People didn't think for themselves, they just followed the social media buzz and hoped for a "follow back." Kyle McMahon, a positivity activist and blogger, also observes this overuse of technology: "We aren't experiencing life. We're losing moments with every tap . . . We may be physically present with our friends . . . but we're texting someone else," he says.

I suggested to a friend that she put her phone away, and she retorted by saying, "When I'm older, I want to remember this!" Yes, it's important to document our lives and take photos so that we can reminisce, but when taking photos for the memories becomes taking photos for speculation or attention on social media, we need to draw a line. When did taking pictures for the memories become taking pictures for the likes, retweets or followers? When did a photo that says "We're having a great time!" turn into one that says, "Everyone look at me because I'm out and you're not!"?

Caroline Tell, an editorial consultant, offers a possible solution for the overuse of cellphones in our technological culture: "Maybe the best way to curb cell phone overuse is by preying on people's social insecurities. In some circles, being inaccessible is a status symbol." Maybe we need to glorify cellphone abstinence to create an environment where putting our phones down is celebrated. An easier approach to the problem is by just putting our phones down. Turning them off. We don't need some drastic, radical change to lessen the use of technology. The solution is easy, and it starts by pressing a simple button.

Sources

"Could We Disconnect For Just A Moment?" The Huffington Post.
"Step Away From the Phone!" The New York Times.

5 #SelfieNation

by Alyssa G. (2015)

Teenage interests seem to come and go. However, there is one trend that seems to be sticking—the selfie. A selfie, as defined by Merriam-Webster, is an image of one taken by oneself using a digital camera, especially for posting on social networks. Over the past few years, selfies have become increasingly popular amongst teenagers, and it's nearly impossible to go on any social media outlets without seeing a photo of a young girl showing off her 'outfit of the day' (or #OOTD) in the mirror, or of a shirtless guy grinning into the camera post-workout.

Due to the popularity of the selfie, older generations are labeling Generation Z as narcissistic—and apparently, selfies are to blame. Erin Ryan, a writer for Jezebel, even went as far as to call them a 'cry for help'. "Selfies aren't empowering; they're a high tech reflection of the way society teaches women that their most important quality is their physical attractiveness," Ryan wrote on her blog article. "Young women take selfies because they don't derive their sense of worth from themselves, they rely on others to bestow their self-worth on them—just as they've been taught," Ryan continued, not only further promoting the stereotype that teenage girls are constantly asking for attention, but also ignoring the high percentage of males that take selfies.

Personally, I find no fault in selfies. They are a form of expression and self-empowerment, in which one feels confident enough to take a picture of oneself and share it with their friends and followers. As argued by New York Times technology reporter, Jenna Wortham, selfies help to record one's daily doings, and how they're feeling at the moment. "Rather than dismissing the trend as a side effect of digital culture or a sad form of exhibitionism, maybe we're better off seeing selfies for what they are at their best—a kind of visual diary, a way to mark our short existence and hold it up to others as proof that we were here," Wortham stated in her 2013 article, "My Selfie, Myself."

Out of the 175 pictures on my Instagram, around half are selfies. Despite the likelihood of being labeled a narcissist, I take pride in the fact that I am able to feel confident enough to share my appearance with hundreds of people. In a generation where being insecure is the norm, selfies act as a getaway. People are allowed to drop the majority of negative thoughts surrounding their appearance, and concentrate on the features they like. Self-confidence, in any form, shouldn't be ridiculed. My advice to readers? Acquaint yourself with the front camera—selfies are here to stay, and for good reason.

Sources

Ryan, Erin. "Selfies Aren't Empowering. They're a Cry for Help." Jezebel. N.p., 21 Nov. 2013. Web. 01 Mar. 2015.

Wortham, Jenna. "My Selfie, Myself." The New York Times. The New York Times, 19 Oct. 2013. Web. 01 Mar. 2015.

6 China Needs Freedom of Information

by Anonymous, 17 (2019)

(Note: This student asked us to keep their name confidential because of the political sensitivity of the topic.)

China is the world's second largest economy. People marvel at its newly-built highways, skyscrapers, and airports, but few know that, while modernizing the country, the Chinese government has also built a Great Firewall on the internet, blocking Western and American websites they deem dangerous to the Chinese minds.

I and my fellow 1.4 billion Chinese citizens are victims of that Wall.

The Great Firewall is blocking the free flow of information into China. When you try to get on The New York Times, The Washington Post or Google, you'd usually get a message that says, "system error." When you try to search some politically sensitive content, such as Taiwan, Tibet or "June 4th," the message could even be threatening: "The content you are searching for is illegal. Report anyone posting such content." My government is afraid of anything on and off the internet that goes against it, even mild criticism.

Yet, some have found a magic tool, a VPN, to go around the information control. A VPN is a computer system that can be used to break free from the Great Fire Wall and is being used as a secret tunnel to get to websites outside of China. Many of my schoolmates are using it to get on to Instagram or YouTube, and I use it to read American newspapers. But it stopped working just recently when the Chinese National People's Congress was in session. I was almost kicked out of WeChat for my "crime" of trying repeatedly to open a New York Times link my tutor sent me from America.

What is tragic is most Chinese don't even know what they are missing out on. On the surface, they are pretty self-sufficient. They use Weibo, so no need for Twitter. They use WeChat, so Facebook can shut its book. They have Bilibili, so YouTube is useless. They have Baidu, so Google can go away. But there is a fundamental difference between the American sites and their Chinese counterparts—our lack of freedom to access information. What we have is what our government allows us to read, to listen to and to watch. But what about our right to the free flow of information?

China may have the fastest 5G networks powered by Western technologies, but it does not afford its citizens basic human rights, and Western trade negotiators should raise this issue when discussing tariffs with our government. The Western countries should put pressure on Beijing to loosen up its political control over its people.

An enlightened mind is a well-informed one. We young Chinese don't want to be benighted in the Internet age. So help us.

Sources

Perlroth, Nicole. "China Is Said to Use Powerful New Weapon to Censor Internet." The New York Times, April 10, 2015.

Wu, Tim. "China's Online Censorship Stifles Trade, Too." The New York Times, Feb. 4, 2019.

7 Spreading Hatred is Not the Answer

by Adrianna N. (2014)

"Cisgender people's opinions don't matter in conversations about gender and sexuality."

"White people have been oppressing people of color for years; they can handle being picked on and having their rights taken away."

"It's time for men to realize that females are the dominant sex."

In the hustle and bustle of moving civil rights forward and spreading tolerance, too many people tend to move backward instead. The above comments were found on social media websites (Facebook, Reddit and Tumblr), written by users from what is frequently viewed as the most accepting demographic: the 18-25-year-old age group, or "Generation X" ("A Portrait of 'Generation Next' ").

One would most likely expect a carefree "let's all be nice to everyone" attitude from people of this generation, but surprisingly, a large handful of these young adults use hatred of privileged or already widely accepted groups as a means of fueling their own fight for civil rights.

Just a few minutes on Tumblr, a popular blogging website, will reveal hundreds of user-written posts encouraging "cisphobia," or the hatred of people who identify with the gender they were assigned at birth; cisphobia is meant to motivate others to be more accepting of those who are transgender or fluidgender.

Other social media users refuse to even talk to males if they are cisgender, heterosexual, white, or all of the above, simply because their opinions have traditionally held the most weight. Some claim that white people should no longer be allowed to hold positions of power, because "it's time to let people of color have a chance"—a whole new and extreme take on affirmative action (Leonhardt).

People who participate in this unusual form of discrimination genuinely believe that they're helping to eradicate homophobia, transphobia, racism, and other common forms of intolerance. In reality, they're only expanding the gap between themselves and acceptance by putting themselves in a negative light.

It is contradictory for someone to demand equality while wishing someone else's rights away. True equality is giving everybody the same rights and the same amount of kindness, regardless of race, sex, gender orientation, sexuality, or culture. Will true equality ever be reached? Right now, we don't know—but spreading hatred is not the answer.

Sources

Leonhardt. David. "Rethinking Affirmative Action." The New York Times. 13 Oct. 2012. Web. 16 March 2013.

"A Portrait of 'Generation Next.' " Pew Research Center for the People and the Press. Pew Research Center. 9 Jan. 2007. Web. 16 March 2014.

Teenage Life Offline

“The best lessons in life come from wandering off the paved path to explore.”

“Messy people are willing to challenge the conventional norm.”

“How should I, an Asian-American, raise my future children?”

8 The Wonders of Wandering

by Lucas Schroeder (2014)

Nowadays, we have instant access to information about what's happening halfway around the world. We can see tanks rolling down the streets of Ukraine, marvel at Olympians in Sochi, and watch celebrities glide down the red carpet in Hollywood from flickering screens in our living rooms. The world seems small, but as Mark Twain observed, "Broad, wholesome, charitable views of men and things cannot be acquired by vegetating in one little corner of the earth all one's lifetime."

The best lessons in life come from wandering off the paved paths to explore. I've spent over eight months wandering across America in my family's minivan. Along the way, I picked cotton with a farmer in Virginia, protected my fry bread from a pack of hungry dogs on an Indian reservation in New Mexico, and rode a stubborn horse named Prince with a rodeo stuntman in Wyoming. Interacting with mustachioed cowboys and sun-weathered mountain climbers along the way helped me learn so much more about other cultures than I'd ever have learned sitting at home.

According to a recent study, benefits of travel start not long after you leave home. In fact, after only a day or so of travel, almost 90% of people have significant drops in stress levels, according to Chris Erskine of the L.A. Times. In addition, researchers have proven that experiencing new cultures actually opens up our minds. By seeing cultural differences, travelers are "more willing to realize that there are different (and equally valid) ways of interpreting the world," says author Jonah Lehrer. Stepping outside of one's familiar bubble can be confusing but it also makes us more creative. Wandering out of our comfort zone to explore doesn't just get us a suntan and souvenirs; it helps us gain a new perspective, engage with new people, and makes us more adaptable.

Trying a bowl of gumbo in Louisiana, huckleberry pie in Montana, or fried okra in Virginia isn't just fun; it makes your mind more aware of the present moment. Scientists have found that such unique experiences open our minds to different ways of thinking.

As Jonah Lehrer explains, "A bit of distance helps loosen the chains of cognition, making it easier to see something new in the old."

When we immerse ourselves fully in unfamiliar surroundings, we're more likely to have wonderful ah-ha moments. It's the journey that matters, not the destination. Whether you end up wandering through swaying stalks of corn, peering up at sequoias scraping the sky, or dodging spiky saguaro cacti, you'll realize that the best way to fully understand life is by exploring. Let yourself wander a bit because, "Not all who wander are lost."

Sources

Erskine, Chris. "Travel Is the Best Medicine, Study Finds." Los Angeles Times, 17 Dec. 2013. Web. 10 March 2014.

Lehrer, Jonah. "Why We Travel." ScienceBlogs, 10 Dec. 2009. Web. 10 March 2014.

Parker-Pope, Tara. "How Vacations Affect Your Happiness." How Vacations Affect Your Happiness Comments. The New York Times, 18 Feb. 2010. Web. 12 March 2014.

9 The Life-Changing Magic of Being Messy

by Isabel Hwang, 17 (2019)

You might have a "messy" friend or family member. You can't help but sigh at the chaos of their room—clean and dirty laundry mixed together. Odds are it'll be difficult to walk two feet without encountering an empty chip bag. Gross? Yes. Bad? Not necessarily.

As a stereotypically "messy" person myself, I've received my own share of scorn. Living in a boarding school, I'm obligated to keep my room nice and tidy, ready for visitors and as a model to underclassmen. Monday room inspections are the norm, and faculty members have sometimes passively, sometimes aggressively, urged my roommate and me to clean up. For these purposes, I used to harbor a 24 x 24 x 24 cardboard box in which I'd stuff everything on Monday mornings and empty it out later that evening. Now, I just throw everything downstairs into the communal storage. Out of sight, out of mind.

As much judgment as we get for our clutter, research has shown that messiness can be a sign of creativity and openness. In the NYT article "It's Not 'Mess.' It's Creativity," Kathleen D. Vohs' study of messiness serves as a rare champion for us less-than-neat people. In her study, she gathered a group of subjects in a tidy room and another in a messy room. When each subject had to choose between a "classic" or "new" smoothie on a fake menu, the subjects in the tidy room chose "classic" while subjects in the messy room chose the "new" smoothies. This shows that "people greatly preferred convention in the tidy room and novelty in the messy room." In addition, Vohs revealed that messy people were more creative. So, what does this mean?

Messy people are willing to challenge the conventional norm. They aren't confined to the status quo. In a growing age where minimalism seems to be taking the world by storm, we must remember that there is beauty in chaos. Although a University of Michigan study warns that some people might take one look at your messy desk and view you as "lazy" or "neurotic," we must remember the people who challenge the old ways of being are some of our greatest innovators. After all, Albert Einstein, Mark Twain, Steve Jobs, and Mark Zuckerberg famously harbored hideously disorganized workplaces.

So, when you see a scatter of papers, laundry, and old food containers, don't rush out to buy your child, friend, or roommate "The Life-Changing Magic of Tidying Up." Instead, appreciate that your acquaintance might be "sparking joy" by channeling their creativity differently.

Sources

Eichenstein, Izzy. "Albert Einstein, Mark Twain & Steve Jobs: The Messy Desk Link." The LAX Morning Minute, Word Press, 19 Oct. 2013.

Vohs, Kathleen. "Tidy Desk or Messy Desk? Each Has Its Benefits." Association for Psychological Science, 6 Aug. 2013.

Vohs, Kathleen D. "It's Not 'Mess.' It's Creativity." The New York Times, 13 Sept. 2013.

Wadley, Jared. "Is Your Office Messy? If So, You May Be Seen as Uncaring, Neurotic." Michigan News, The University of Michigan, 27 Nov. 2018.

Weinswig, Deborah. "Millennials Go Minimal: The Decluttering Lifestyle Trend That Is Taking Over." Forbes, 7 Sept. 2016.

10 Tiger Parenting: An Angel in Disguise

by Michelle Twan, 17 (2019)

I used to not want to be Asian.

My non-Asian friends' parents were affectionate and never threatened them because of a "B." Mine were tiger parents, and I despised it. But when they transitioned to a more Western approach to parenting, I saw the effects and changed my mind.

My sister, who's 11 years older, was raised heavily with tiger parenting, or the authoritarian approach–harsh punishments, little nurturing. Though brutal, it was understandable: my parents wanted their child to have a better life, and this was how they were raised themselves. My sister ended up successful—but she suffered because of the tremendous pressure placed on her.

I was also raised with tiger parenting, but my parents became less authoritarian after my sister got into dental school. I'm more emotionally stable than my oldest sister was at my age, but my grades and SAT score are significantly less impressive. Was it because of how I was raised? What would've happened if I hadn't experienced any tiger parenting? Would I have been less motivated? Less worried about my future? If possible, maybe even less intelligent?

This leads me to ask: how should I, an Asian-American, raise my future children?

It's a question that many American children of Asian immigrants ask. Some Asian-Americans are traumatized by tiger parenting, but it's part of our tradition, our culture. A New York Times article reports that "we're largely abandoning traditional Asian parenting styles in favor of a modern, Western approach focused on developing open and warm relationships with our children," but is that actually good? I want my children to be raised with love, but also with a strict regime that emphasizes the importance of education—a cornerstone of tiger parenting. Tiger parenting leads to success. Asian-Americans attend prestigious universities in large numbers and make up "12 percent of the professional workforce while making up only 5.6 percent of the U.S. population," my sister included. Tiger parents are intimidating, but effective.

That's why I want to raise my children through tiger parenting—with enough love to minimize emotional scars but still ensure success: a mix of me and my sister. Other Asian-Americans should consider this, too; after all, with each successive generation, immigrant children do worse, and the absence of tiger parenting is partly to blame. I don't want my parents' sacrifices and hardships to be in vain because I didn't raise successful, intelligent, "Asian" children, and I know the same goes for other Asian-Americans. We're Americans, but we don't need to abandon our traditional method of raising children. With tweaks, tiger parenting doesn't have to be abhorred—it can be embraced and appreciated.

Sources

Gee, Buck, and Denise Peck. "Asian Americans Are the Least Likely Group in the U.S. to Be Promoted to Management." Harvard Business Review, 31 May 2018.

Park, Ryan. "The Last of the Tiger Parents." The New York Times, 22 June 2018.

Weissbourd, Richard. "Why Do Immigrant Children Struggle More Than Their Parents Did?" The New Republic, 25 Feb. 2002.

11 To Bae or Not To Bae

by Paula L. (2015)

"Then Becky was like you're so ratchet and then I was like do you want to go—"

It is sadly not surprising that this conversation took place in a local house of learning, my high school. It would be more startling if verbs and adjectives that are used in more articulate conversations were employed.

In a country that embodies freedom of speech, America is getting lax in its everyday dialogue. People are resorting to slang more frequently, making their language seem sloppy. They are echoing expressions from popular music or television that wouldn't normally be used. With 470,000 entries in the Merriam-Webster Dictionary, society still limits self-expression by embracing frivolous words.

Slang is taking the easy way out by conveying a person's ideas in a generalized, overused format. The Chicago Tribune article, "Say What?", quotes Dave Wilton of wordorigins.org, who claims '"By sharing an 'in' vocabulary, a group can distinguish itself from the wider culture . . . Teens, for example, can use slang to separate themselves from adults or from other teen cliques"' (Park, Vinson). That's all well and good, but it is getting to a point where we are conditioned to say the right thing in one situation and a completely different one somewhere else. The "in" vocabulary is confining people to the group's concept instead of asserting their feelings in better terms. A girl wouldn't ordinarily tell her friend that she thought he is a dear friend that she greatly appreciates; no, she would simply call him BAE. "Before Anyone Else" is so overly used that the sentiment is completely lost. Society is going through the motions of what is in style and accepted.

Any language fluctuates with the times. A perceptive metaphor from New York Times article, "Slang for the Ages" by Kory Stamper, states "English is fluid and enduring; not a mountain, but an ocean. A word may drift through time from one current of English to another" (Stamper). We use words in all different situations to get various points across. Don't let evolving times diminish meaningful conversations to "wus'sup bro". Embrace individuality and speak what's on your mind. In an ocean of words, don't swim in the commonplace tidal pool; revel in the exhilarating waves.

In George Orwell's dystopian novel, 1984, language and society are moving in an alarming direction. The language Newspeak's goal is "every concept that can ever be needed will be expressed by exactly one word, with its meaning rigidly defined" (Orwell 46). In our society, there are hundreds of thousands of words at our disposal and freedom of speech is in our hands. We are truly fortunate to have it. So use those words and don't revert to Newspeak!

Sources

Orwell, George. 1984. New York: Signet Classic, 1950. Print.

Park, Morgan, and Vinson, Emanuel. "Say What?" The Chicago Tribune. 14 May 2009. Web. 3 March 2015. http://articles.chicagotribune.com/2009-05-14/news/0905170167_1_slang-teens-oxford-english-dictionary

Stamper, Kory. "Slang for the Ages." New York Times. 3 Oct. 2014. Web. 3 March 2015. http://www.nytimes.com/2014/10/04/opinion/slang-for-the-ages.html?_r=0

12 Moving Forwards: Stopping Volunteer Tourism

by Jack Jian Kai Zhang, 16 (2019)

No Good Samaritan would intentionally do harm to the 69 million refugees and 766 million individuals living in extreme poverty around the world. Unfortunately, this happens all too frequently. "Voluntourists" are volunteers—often from the West—who pay companies to arrange short-term charity work in poor countries, ostensibly to assist the less fortunate. I've seen plenty of my peers' pictures on these trips. Voluntourists, my friends included, may have noble intentions with volunteering abroad, but they represent the commercial corruption of charity and inadvertently reinforce the imperial conceptions of foreign cultures that contributed to global wealth inequality in the first place. We, both as students and as global citizens, ought to avoid falling into the feel-good trap of direct foreign volunteering.

Firstly, voluntourism agencies divert money from those who need it most. Over two billion dollars are spent each year on agency-arranged voluntourism trips. This sum nearly quadruples the total U.S. economic assistance in 2017 to South Sudan, Syria, and the Democratic Republic of the Congo—all countries with severe humanitarian crises. And yet, despite massive spending on voluntourism, proportionally little good comes of it: at one major voluntourism agency, less than a third of the money spent ultimately reaches communities in need. The rest disappears into administrative costs, advertising spending, and shareholders' pockets. In terms of financial efficiency, voluntourism falls short.

Even if the financial frictions to foreign volunteering were justified, it remains far from clear that voluntourists are actually able to provide the assistance that they intend to give. For example, the introduction of short-term volunteers to orphaned children can easily cause serious developmental harm. The children, often looking for long-term emotional attachment, end up repeatedly losing their short-term volunteer friends. Indeed, while the United Nations Refugee Agency lists fundraising, planned gifts, and one-time donations under its "How to Help" page, directly volunteering in orphanages is notably absent.

Still, proponents of voluntourism argue that it is better than nothing: costly, yes, but nevertheless a form of much-needed assistance to the less fortunate. However, this defense highlights a less obvious, and arguably more fundamental, issue with voluntourism: its roots in a colonial psyche. The notion that untrained Westerners can meaningfully better foreign communities is both unrealistic and based on an unspoken Western myth of superiority. It is as if foreign cultures will be elevated by speaking Western languages, by conforming to Western culture, and with the direct assistance of amateur Western volunteers. Voluntourism paints a picture of inferiority and dependence for givers and receivers of voluntourism alike. Eliminating this form of international support, which reinforces imperialist visions of "saving" the Global South, will contribute to a future based on mutual respect and solidarity instead of pity and reliance.

Sources

Bearak, Max and Lazaro Gamio. "The U.S. Foreign Aid Budget, Visualized." The Washington Post, 18 Oct. 2016.

Blackledge, Sam. "In Defence of 'Voluntourists.'" The Guardian, 25 Feb. 2013.

Hartman, Eric, Cody Morris Paris, and Brandon Blache-Cohen. "Fair Trade Learning: Ethical Standards for Community-Engaged International Volunteer Tourism." Tourism and Hospitality Research, vol. 14, no. 1-2, 10 June 2014, p. 108-116.

"How to Help." USA for UNHCR: The UN Refugee Agency, 2018.

Howton, Elizabeth. "Nearly Half the World Lives on Less than $5.50 a Day." The World Bank, 17 Oct. 2018.

"Refugee Facts." USA for UNHCR: The UN Refugee Agency, 2018.

Rosenberg, Tina. "How to Really Help Children Abroad." The New York Times, 23 Oct. 2018.

Wesby, Maya. "The Exploitative Selfishness of Volunteering Abroad." Newsweek, 18 Aug. 2018.

"Where Does the Money Go?" Projects Abroad, 2014.

School

“I realize I have been fed a filtered version of history all my life.”

“The lockdowns I’ve been taught over and over again, sitting in the dark, actually tell future active shooters exactly where we’re going to be—cornered.”

“We should not be desperately trying to handle the stress of this system. We should be changing the system itself.”

13 In Three and a Half Hours, an Alarm Will Go Off

by Konrad U. and Che E. (2019)

In three and a half hours, an alarm will go off, and one of the authors of this article will drag himself out of bed, plop his head in a bowl of cereal, and dive into a swimming pool. The other has a luxurious five hours to look forward to, but don't worry, he'll pay for it tomorrow night; that science fair project won't finish itself, after all.

We are both in high school. We are both juniors. And we both have yet to go to bed.

Welcome to a normal Monday morning.

This is not an anomaly. Sleep deprivation is pervasive in high schools across the country. Fewer than 20 percent of high school students get the recommended nine hours of sleep they need each night, and two-thirds are classified as severely sleep deprived. And yet, just this past fall, schools in New York City started the school day 40 minutes early to accommodate more extracurricular activities, despite evidence indicating that starting school later could reduce teen car accidents by 65 to 70 percent. What are we doing to our students?

Prior to the 1950s, most scientists saw sleep as simply a period during which the brain was recuperating from the constant "bombardment" of information humans receive every day—not necessarily as a fundamental ingredient in a person's well-being. But by the 1990s, studies had conclusively shown that sleep deprivation is a significant problem, and is now considered a public health epidemic by the CDC. Sleep deprivation has been linked to a higher risk of obesity, diabetes, and suicide, not to mention the well known losses in productivity and alertness students experience throughout a normal school day.

As national concern grows over the lagging educational standards of schools in the United States, our natural inclination is to load teens with harder coursework, more challenging extracurriculars and earlier start times. But when the recommended sleep for teens is unheard of in most high schools, enabling students to get more rest becomes not only a priority but an imperative. For many of our high school peers, even severe sleep deprivation (seven hours or fewer) is incredibly attractive when compared to the status quo. It is therefore baffling when discussions on how to improve student performance rarely center on making students themselves healthier and more well rested. Until educators and regulators recognize their actions' effect on students' sleep patterns, students will be stuck trying to forever make up for lost sleep. If we want the future leaders of our nation to continue to innovate, thrive and make the world a better place, they are going to need a good night's sleep.

Sources

Brody, Jane. "Hard Lesson in Sleep for Teenagers." The New York Times. 20 Oct. 2014.

Lahey, Jessica. "Students Aren't Getting Enough Sleep—School Starts Too Early." The Atlantic, 25 Aug. 2014.

Dement, William C . "The Study of Human Sleep: A Historical Perspective." Thorax, 1 October 1998.

Colten HR, Altevogt BM, editors. "Sleep Disorders and Sleep Deprivation: An Unmet Public Health Problem." Institute of Medicine (US) Committee on Sleep Medicine and Research, 2006.

14 The 4th R: Real Life

by Jason Schnall, 16 (2018)

Who's to blame for ballooning credit card debt and student loans? The public education system, perhaps. American high school students can recite Shakespeare's sonnets, derive advanced calculus theorems, and explain the Chinese spheres of influence. Yet these same students know little to nothing about economics and personal finance. They know of income tax only as the fifth square on the Monopoly board.

Currently, only five states—Alabama, Missouri, Tennessee, Utah and Virginia—require personal finance courses for high school students. The results speak for themselves: four of these states rank in the top 20 of best average credit card debt. This is a logical correlation. Learning about debt will help someone stay out of it. Yet economists continually blame consumerism and tactics of credit card companies rather than addressing the cause: a fundamental void in our education system.

When students graduate high school, they are thrust into adulthood, whether they join the work force or pursue higher education. They assume immense financial responsibilities almost immediately. How can the government expect 19-year-olds to complete tax forms if they've never learned about them in school? Young adults who lack basic knowledge of economics and personal finance are vulnerable to fraud, debt, commercialism and worse.

In the 2012 New York Times article "Back to Classroom for Skills not Taught in High School," Matthew R. Warren discusses a personal finance course in the Bronx where students learn vital information not taught in their high schools. Warren quotes 22-year-old student Regina Rice, "I can't manage my money . . . Yesterday, I bought two pairs of headphones, and I don't even know why."

Ideally, parents with lifelong experience would teach their children about personal finance. But, 61 percent of parents only discuss money when prompted by their children. The average American parent lacks the knowledge necessary to teach this information, as many of them live in severe debt themselves, including the 32 percent of U.S. households that carry credit card debt.

The solution? A required course—Personal Finance and the Modern Economy—taught to second-semester high school seniors. It's vital that students learn basic information about taxes, insurance, mortgages, credit, loans, personal banking, consumerism and the stock market before they are forced to learn it the hard way.

Financial literacy should not be a privilege reserved for children of the Wall Street elite. It is a skill that must be taught, just as vital in today's economy as reading, writing and arithmetic. So why do we keep treating it like an elective?

Sources

"Average Credit Card Debt in America: 2017 Facts & Figures." ValuePenguin, ValuePenguin, 21 March 2018.

Desjardins, Jeff. "Chart: Are Today's Students Prepared to Make Financial Decisions?" Visual Capitalist, 29 Sept. 2017.

"T. Rowe Price: Parents Are Likely To Pass Down Good And Bad Financial Habits To Their Kids." T. Rowe Price, 23 March 2017.

Warren, Mathew R. "Financial Literacy Class Offers Skills Not Taught in School." The New York Times, 27 Jan. 2012.

15 Gym Class Villains

by Nora Berry, 17, and Chase Moriarty, 17 (2016)

Each year, high school students take on a new set of classes, more challenging and demanding than last year's. Geometry leads to algebra which gives way to statistics and calculus. Students are expected to adapt to and grow with the increased difficulty in all subjects. Or almost all subjects—physical education hasn't changed in generations, mired in outdated tradition. Teaching students the value of a healthy lifestyle and the power of teamwork remains critical to their success in life. However, an unimaginative curriculum of forced laps and overly aggressive games fails to accomplish much beyond boredom and exclusion. Like other curricula, physical education should be updated to support and reflect the complexity and individuality of current day adolescents.

One aspect of traditional physical education most in need of updating is the built-in threat of judgment and ridicule. In sports such as speedball and volleyball, boys are mocked for not being masculine enough while girls are criticized for getting too sweaty. Sportswriter Selena Roberts accounts in her New York Times article that "in men's locker rooms, gay slurs are the ultimate insults to raging manhood." Gym teachers facilitate this atmosphere by continuing to conduct fitness tests and allow captain-selected teams. Those who are less proficient find themselves ostracized by their sportier peers. Gym teachers then compound the problem by grading students based on skill rather than effort. As if being weighed in front of your classmates isn't punishment enough, your G.P.A. suffers as well.

While gym class would seem a natural arena for competition, perhaps students would benefit from its absence. P.E. teachers should give students more voice and provide more options, giving opportunities to students who do not perform well in rigorous, ultracompetitive environments. Students could explore their athleticism in a less cutthroat way, such as through a weight training program or archery.

Just as the school would not put every student in a remedial math class and then hold a contest to see who could solve problems aloud, why should everyone be forced to compete at dodge ball? Students should be developing a lifelong interest in healthy physical activity. The National Institute of Diabetes reports "among young people ages 2 to 19, about 32 percent are overweight or obese." Today's physical education classes must address this.

For the good of students, physical education must evolve. Gym should be engaging and inclusive of varying skill levels. Instruction should address each student's individual needs and abilities, just as in other educational classes. Students need opportunities to participate without fear of humiliation. Physical education has faltered in its mission, but with some updating, it could have the profound and lasting effect of making students healthier and happier.

Sources

Roberts, Selena. "Homophobia Is Alive in Men's Locker Rooms." The New York Times. 28 Oct. 2005.

"Overweight and Obesity Statistics." The National Institute of Diabetes and Digestive and Kidney Diseases.

16 Accountability-Based Testing Is Broken

by Alan Peng, 17 (2018)

In 2015, eleven teachers were convicted of racketeering and other crimes in the infamous Atlanta Public Schools cheating scandal, in which "inordinate pressure" from top administrators to meet standardized test score targets or face severe consequences led the teachers to cheat on state standardized tests. Sadly, such cases of coordinated, large-scale cheating are surprisingly pervasive, underscoring the undue importance attached to standardized test results. These test results are used in an admirable effort at accountability, but the process of accountability via standardized testing is now deeply flawed. Testing has evolved into an industry, a game for test companies and policymakers; everyone benefits—except the students and educators, who are just cogs in the machine.

For instance, as part of the process, teachers are forced to spend more and more time "teaching to the test," wasting valuable instruction time. This wouldn't be such an issue if the tests are high-quality or instructive, but they aren't, for a variety of reasons. First, they're unfair. Research has shown that the tests nontrivially discriminate against different races and socioeconomic backgrounds. Consequently, since standardized tests compare schools and districts of all different backgrounds, affluent schools are rewarded and struggling schools are punished.

Second, they're inaccurate. Standardized tests often involve multiple errors or ridiculous content; for instance, the test company Pearson has occasionally misprinted tests, misplaced or misgraded answer sheets, and faced major technical issues. In 2012, an absurd story involving an anthropomorphic pineapple in a contrived remake of "The Tortoise and the Hare" graced the desks of middle schoolers across several states, with senseless questions that stumped even teachers. Clearly, these tests are managed not by educational experts, but by profit-seeking companies.

But most importantly, they test for the wrong things. With their pervasive focus on multiple choice and shallow thinking, standardized tests ignore creativity, grit and depth of understanding, thus turning students into robots. The real world requires deep, innovative thinkers, but tests encourage students to automatize themselves.

Another oft-cited reason for testing is that their objective results allow instructors to better address their students' needs. However, these teachers have been trained professionally, usually have known the students in a much more personal, holistic and genuine context for several months, and often don't even get the results back before the end of the year, and so this argument doesn't hold much water.

Accountability-based testing can still be salvaged. Placing more control in the hands of educators would allow them to rework tests to be more pedagogically meaningful, and results should only be interpreted with the whole context in mind. Otherwise schools will just turn into factories for producing high test scores.

Sources

Chapman, Ben, and Rachel Monahan. "Talking Pineapple Question on State Exam Stumps . . . Everyone!" New York Daily News, 20 April 2012.

"How Useful Are Standardized Tests?" The New York Times, 17 Feb. 2015.

"Racial Bias Built into Tests." FairTest.

Strauss, Valerie. "How and Why Convicted Atlanta Teachers Cheated on Standardized Tests." The Washington Post, 1 April 2015.

Strauss, Valerie. "Pearson's History of Testing Problems - a List." The Washington Post, 21 April 2016.

17 Stopping Bullets With Locked Doors and Silence Is Already Pulling the Trigger

by Daina Kalnina, 15 (2017)

It has become very familiar for high-school students to practice the infamous level-three lockdown. In all cases, we all share the semi-nervous chuckle of "wow, maybe we get Swiss-cheesed today" and sit in a corner, stare at our phones and text our friends. Only very recently, after a vivid dream—more a nightmare—of a school shooting, did I realize that sitting in the dark and stopping bullets with locked doors and silence is the exact opposite of what one would want to do. It wasn't until I stumbled upon the fact that the "people shot and killed in the Columbine library sat there for five minutes before the shooters entered and shot them." My school is full of able-bodied kids, and surprisingly, a great chunk that has had experience with self-defense and even marksman training. So why sit and wait?

To say that the drills today are relevant is a mistake. They do more than just offer very little protection; they also endanger students and teachers more so than ever before. The lockdowns I've been taught over and over again, sitting in the dark, actually tell future active shooters exactly where we're going to be—cornered. Moreover, in The New York Times article, "In Shift, Police Advise Taking an Active Role to Counter Mass Attacks," studies conducted by law enforcement in the Virginia Tech shooting showed that "the students and teacher blocked the door with a heavy desk and held it in place, [the shooter] could not get in, and everyone lived," compared to those that tried to "hide or play dead," in which almost all were shot or died. It is shown more clearly here than ever that by making the vital choice to barricade and move as a means of security will utilize finite time better and save lives.

Many educators and parents have questioned the authenticity and have begun to develop alternatives for active-shooter lockdowns. The ALICE project is one such adaptation. Developed by a former SWAT officer Greg

Cane, ALICE stands for alert, lockdown, inform, counter, evacuate. It provides specialized tactics for K-12 and higher education schools. Fundamentally, a moving target is harder to get an aim on than a stationary one. That same difference marks ALICE's method from the old one; it encourages movement, distraction and most importantly, it encourages direct action from students and teachers. This significantly decreases the number of lives lost and helps me sleep a little bit better at night knowing that if the time ever comes, I'm not idly waiting to become Swiss cheese.

It's unnerving that the students of this country must learn how to cope with active shooters.

It's even more unnerving that current procedures say that they should sit, wait and die.

Sources

Lupkin, Sydney. "School Safety Experts Disagree on Lock Down Procedures." ABC News. ABC News Network, 16 Dec. 2012. Web. Mar. 2017.

Cane, Greg. "Active Shooter Response Training—ALICE" ALICE Training Institute. ALICE, n.d. Web. Mar. 2017.

Goode, Erica. "In Shift, Police Advise Taking an Active Role to Counter Mass Attacks." The New York Times. The New York Times, 06 Apr. 2013. Web. Mar. 2017.

18 Why We Should Teach The Truth About American History

by Patrick Wang, 16 (2019)

The bell rings, and I barely make it into my AP U.S. History class. I look up at the board: "Today's Topic: Slavery." I do not think much about it because slavery has been a part of the Georgia curriculum since elementary school. What more could I possibly need to learn about? Yet, as I read through sickening excerpts of "Uncle Tom's Cabin" and watch clips of "Twelve Years a Slave," I can feel the horror building up inside me. I am confronted by my own ignorance, the cruel reality of history clashing with my own sugar-coated understanding. I realize that I have been fed a filtered version of history all my life. In the end, however, I am thankful for the opportunity to learn the truth in my AP U.S. history class, because for millions of other students, the truth is a privilege denied in the name of "patriotism."

In 2015, College Board's AP U.S. History course came under fire for "painting American history in too negative a light." Conservative critics charged that the framework of the course was "biased and unpatriotic," with GOP presidential candidate Ben Carson even calling the course "so anti-American that students who completed it would be ready to sign up for ISIS." Many states such as Texas and Georgia even threatened to pull the course all together. Caving under pressure, the College Board changed the AP U.S. History framework to include a new emphasis on "American exceptionalism."

This controversy brings to light the U.S.'s inability to own up to its past. Whether we like it or not, the U.S. is a country built upon not just democracy but exploitation and injustice. Events like the My Lai massacre and the slave trade are scary and real. We can not casually sweep the ugly pieces of history under the rug and hope that our rosy facade continues to fool the next generation into being "patriotic." Patriotism is not the pride you feel when you believe that your country has done no wrong. Patriotism is the pride you feel when you know that your country is on the present journey to righting its past wrongs and preventing future wrongs.

By indoctrinating students with the idea of "American exceptionalism" rather than teaching them the truth about American history, the only people we end up fooling are ourselves. As the Yale professor of American Studies Jon Butler puts it, "America emerged out of many contentious issues. If we understand those issues, [only then can we] figure out how to move forward in the present." Thus, knowing the truth about American history should not be a privilege. It is a right.

Sources

Ganim, Sara. "Making History: Battles Brew over Alleged Bias in Advanced Placement Standards." CNN, 24 Feb. 2015.

Quinlan, Casey. "College Board Caves to Conservative Pressure, Changes AP U.S. History Curriculum." Think Progress, 30 July 2015.

Schlanger, Zoe. "Revised AP U.S. History Standards Will Emphasize American Exceptionalism." Newsweek, 29 July 2015.

Simon, Cecilia Capuzzi. "Taking the Politics Out of American History (and Out of A.P.)." The New York Times, 8 Apr. 2016.

19 The Unspoken Alphabet Problem

by Stephanie Zhang, 14 (2017)

"Lineup in alphabetical order!" my elementary teacher says as we come to a halt; Johnny stops telling his story about the frog he caught last weekend at his grandparents' house while Carlos jumps off the swings midair, hoping to impress the girls today. We all run back to class, forming a line and departing from our adventures in the land of recess. I'm last in line. Every. Day.

The system of alphabetical order in schools must be changed, as a silent bias toward the names starting with letters near the end of the alphabet is causing detrimental effects to our children's psychology due to the subconscious implications of inferiority.

As someone with the last name "Zhang," I still remember the rush of excitement I felt when my teacher read the roll sheet from the bottom to the top—only on special occasions, of course. I remember the condolences the teacher would give, telling me "last but not least!" But I still felt least. This display of alphabetical inequality not only continually provides an unfair disadvantage and feeling of inferiority to the same group of people; it also affects our decisions made later in life.

In the New York Times article "How Inequality Hollows Out the Soul" by Richard Wilkinson and Kate Pickett, it discusses how social inequality allows us to "not only [see] what we knew intuitively—that inequality is divisive and socially corrosive—but that it also damages the individual psyche." If inequality in wealth damages people, why wouldn't inequality in school cause damage as well?

In a recent four-series scientific study in the Journal of Consumer Research conducted by Kurt A. Carlson, assistant professor at Georgetown, and Jacqueline M. Conard, assistant professor at Belmont University, the professors found that those who had last names later in the alphabet reacted quicker to special sale opportunities when offered deals simultaneously.

"We find that the later in the alphabet the first letter of one's childhood surname is, the faster the person acquires items as an adult. We dub this the last name effect . . . it stems from childhood ordering structures that put children with different names in different positions in lines . . . since those late in the alphabet are typically at the end of lines, they compensate by responding quickly to acquisition opportunities," Professor Carlson says.

Alphabetical order is fine for files in cabinets or books in a library or for naming hurricanes. It is not appropriate for organizing people. "There may be no great alternatives to alphabetical order," says Professor Carlson. "But flip it around every now and then. That's a reasonable way to balance things out."

Sources

Gregory, Sean. "How Your Name May Cost You at the Mall." Time, 28 Jan. 2011.

Wilkinson, Richard and Kate Pickett. "How Inequality Hollows Out the Soul." The New York Times, 2 Feb. 2014.

20 Limiting Science Education: Limiting Ourselves

by James Chan, 17 (2019)

We've landed men on the moon, mapped out our genomes, and split atoms, but for the past 20 years, nobody knew why two grapes produced plasma in a microwave. Energy is conserved. Carbon's atomic number is six. The mitochondria is the powerhouse of the cell . . . Throughout my entire high school career, I've heard all of these facts presented to me, but never once have I felt as intrigued as I have from [watching a video about] this bizarre plasma phenomenon.

Welcome to the world of high school science education.

Sadly, my experience mirrors that of others my age. In a New York Times article, when asked to name a change they would make to science classes, high school students across the nation replied, "I'd rather understand than just memorize formulas" and "I'd like more hands-on projects where I would learn something about what I'm doing instead of just memorizing things from a textbook."

For certain, memorization has its uses; repetition can help students master fundamental skills and retain key pieces of information. "Students cannot apply what they understand," William R. Klemm, a professor at Texas A&M University, notes, "if they don't remember it." But too often does repetition end up replacing more meaningful forms of learning. In science education especially, it ends up stifling curiosity and creativity, deterring people from science careers and opportunities.

The truth is that most students in today's schools are rarely exposed to the limits of our knowledge. As a result, many are led to see science as a source of clear, well-defined answers, that every possible question has been solved. They see the rigorous process of inquiry, experimentation, and analysis as two-sentence lines in a textbook. Rote memorization discourages skepticism while encouraging blind, unquestioning acceptance of facts.

Yet these qualities are the opposite of what science embodies. Science is not complete, but ever-evolving. Science is not linear and static, but sporadic and dynamic. Most importantly, science is a process that embodies tackling uncertainty head-on, asking questions that push the boundaries of knowledge. Each answer is never final, but instead provokes new questions that demand new answers. If we never present these aspects of science, how can we excite our students and inspire curiosity? How can we expect innovation and discovery from our students if all we teach them is how to cram?

The solution? Schools must embrace and teach not only what is known, but what is unknown. The role of science teachers is not just to rattle off facts like a broken cassette player, but to challenge students to search beyond what is taught in class. If we continue to teach just memorization, we misrepresent science and ultimately fail to inspire the next generation of innovators.

Sources

Dreifus, Claudia. "Ideas for Improving Science Education." The New York Times, 2 Sept. 2013.

Gorman, James. "When Plasma Becomes Another Fruit of the Vine." The New York Times, 5 Mar. 2019.

Klemm, William. "What Good Is Learning If You Don't Remember It?" Journal of Effective Teaching, 2007.

21 Is It Actually Smart to Sit Still?

by Hannah Amell, 15 (2018)

Some tap pencils relentlessly against desks. Some remain completely unaware of their rapidly bouncing knees or shaking feet. Some stare into space, lost in whatever daydream that is playing out on the board in front of them, unable to see the math problems on it. Some turn to their phones for a source of interaction—a teacher's worst nightmare.

Students are restless. And what do schools require them to do? Sit.

The recent implementation of block scheduling in about 30 percent of American high schools is intended to allow students more time to process information and be productive in class. However, productivity is difficult to measure when, throughout 90 minutes of sitting still, students become restless and disengage, hindering their opportunities to learn and wasting their teachers' time. There could be a simple solution to this problem with multiple benefits: increased movement in the classroom.

Exercise enhances concentration, especially when repeated throughout the day. For many students, walking from one class to another is the only opportunity to move during the school day, and with a block schedule that varies from day to day, physical education class is not the answer.

A high school teacher found after following students for two days that sitting all day left her feeling lethargic and "desperate to move or stretch." She also experienced difficulty paying attention due to prolonged inactivity, claiming she struggled to keep her "mind and body from slipping into oblivion after so many hours of sitting passively." Similar results were found by the Institute of Medicine; children who are regularly active "show greater attention, have faster cognitive processing speed and perform better on standardized academic tests than children who are less active."

The detriments of sitting for long hours of time extend beyond concentration problems; a lack of frequent activity can cause lifelong issues. A study by Stanford University found that long periods of inactivity, specifically sitting, can contribute toward the development of type-2 diabetes, heart disease and obesity.

School requires students to sit for nearly seven hours every day. This disturbs students' education and puts their health at risk. Simply incorporating movement into classroom activities, stretching during class and offering alternatives to sitting still will improve students' grades and health.

School's purpose is to educate students, but the current structure of our schools is an obstacle to students' education. When will school be designed for the students?

Sources

Cruz, Donna De La. "Why Kids Shouldn't Sit Still in Class." The New York Times, 21 March 2017.

James, Julia. "High School Students Sit for Too Long, New Health Research Suggests." Peninsula Press, 10 April 2011.

Strauss, Valerie. "Teacher Spends Two Days as a Student and Is Shocked at What She Learns." The Washington Post, 24 Oct. 2014.

22 Sex Ed and Abortion in America: Hypocrisy at Its Finest

by Sylvia Hollander, 17 (2018)

Abortion is one of the most polarizing topics in the United States. For many on both sides, you're either with them or against them, and unwilling to compromise. But what if there was a way to reduce abortion rates without blocking women from getting them? The answer is simple: better sex education.

For the past few decades there has been a large push to end the abstinence-only sex education implemented by many schools across the U.S. Several studies have found that an abstinence-only education does not work, as it is becoming increasingly unlikely to expect young people to remain abstinent until they are married, considering the increasing age of marriage. There has also been significant evidence that cohesive sex ed classes decrease the chances of unplanned pregnancy and abortion. In theory, abstinence is an idealistic solution, but it has been shown time and time again to be unsuccessful in practice.

One program that has actually shown positive results is the Teen Pregnancy Prevention Program, which is evidence-based and funds a wide variety of organizations working to prevent teen pregnancy. In the past decade the CDC has reported the average teenage birthrate has dropped more than 40 percent, due to the help of the TPP and similar programs.

After defunding the Planned Parenthood budget and closing 81 clinics in Texas, teen abortion rates were found to have risen a significant amount. Meanwhile, Colorado offered free birth control, and teen abortions decreased by 42 percent in just 4 years. This is just one example of how it has been shown that limiting access to family planning services such as Planned Parenthood actually drives up the need for abortions, while providing contraception and informing people of how to be safe drives the need for abortion down. Why is it then that Republican lawmakers continue to slash funding for these organizations?

It would be logical to assume that an administration with a pro-life agenda would be eager to decrease abortions in any way they could, however, this seems to not be the case. Regardless of its proven benefits, the Trump administration canceled funding for 81 projects in the TPP program, while increasing funds for abstinence programs. The fact that the government is ignoring fact-based evidence under the guise of being "pro-life" is appalling. It has been shown that quality sex education is highly beneficial, and if the government truly wants to stop abortions from happening, this is the way to do it. Until then, we need to call them out for their blatant hypocrisy and urge legislators to pay attention to the facts, protect the rights of its citizens and remind others to stay informed.

Sources

Baker, Aspen. "A Better Way to Talk about Abortion." TED: Ideas Worth Spreading, May 2015.

Bassett, Laura. "Teen Abortions Surged In Texas After Republicans Defunded Planned Parenthood." The Huffington Post, 12 July 2017.

Bennet, James. "Opinion | The Gathering Threat to Abortion Rights." The New York Times, The New York Times, 31 Jan. 2018.

Bump, Philip. "Analysis | How America Feels about Abortion." The Washington Post, WP Company, 24 April 2017.

Carroll, Aaron E. "Sex Education Based on Abstinence? There's a Real Absence of Evidence." The New York Times, The New York Times, 22 Aug. 2017.

Forrester, Christina. "The Truth About Christianity And Abortion." The Huffington Post. 19 April 2017.

German Lopez. "Colorado Offered Free Birth Control—and Teen Abortions Fell by 42 Percent." Vox, Vox, 7 July 2014.

"Reproductive Health." Centers for Disease Control and Prevention, Centers for Disease Control and Prevention, 16 Nov. 2017.

"Reproductive Health: Teen Pregnancy." Centers for Disease Control and Prevention, Centers for Disease Control and Prevention, 9 May 2017.

Santelli, John. "Analysis | Abstinence-Only Education Doesn't Work. We're Still Funding It." The Washington Post, WP Company, 21 Aug. 2017.

23 The Korean Dream Is A Korean Tragedy

by Jinha Kim, 15 (2019)

November 16th, 2018. No planes are permitted to land in South Korea for an hour. It's not a national crisis. It's not a terrorist attack. It's just an ordinary day in November except that sixty thousand Korean students take Korea's college entrance exam, the College Scholastic Ability Test. Even the distant noise of a plane landing is an outrageous distraction: the CSAT is the decisive shot for students to achieve their "Korean dream."

The CSAT is the Korean version of the SAT, a yearly exam spanning nine hours and eight subjects. This exam is the culmination of twelve years of study and will impact students' lives for many more. The college a student attends "determines his future for the rest of his life," says Kim Dong Chun, a sociologist at Sungkonghoe University. Lower-ranking colleges graduates have a harder time getting employed as "large conglomerates [tend] to hire people from a specific university" and entry "into a top university is still the key to economic success and social status in Korea."

Given its importance in college admissions, the CSAT pressures students to the extreme. 53 percent of South Koreans students "who confessed to feeling suicidal in 2010 [have] identified inadequate academic performance as the main reason for such thoughts." Jin-yeong, a CSAT retaker, exclaims "when I found out my score was less than what I needed, my heart broke. I felt like I wanted to melt into the ground and disappear." Students like Jin-yeong undergo emotional breakdowns that severely lessen their self-confidence as they face the brutal future of not having a fighting chance at their chosen career.

As a student in Korea who studied in Canada, I am resolute that there is a better alternative education system. Although some assert that standardized tests are most efficient for college admissions, many countries have already moved away from the system. Canadian colleges do not put as much weight on provincial exams and focus more on extracurriculars and students' school lives. Canada's less competitive education system was why I found learning to be fun rather than stressful.

The "Korean Dream" has brainwashed students on what a successful life is: an excellent CSAT score and a prestigious college degree. Contrary to some beliefs that academic pressure is inevitable, students do not deserve this much pressure only to have twelve years of arduous studying judged, possibly poorly, by a single CSAT score. The CSAT—a hierarchical, life-changing test—should be replaced with a less heavily-weighted test, such as the SAT, in the admission process. Colleges should instead acknowledge the importance of extracurriculars such as club activities, and stop determining students solely by standardized scores. It is time that this Korean tragedy ends.

Sources

Choe, Sang Hun. "In South Korea, Students Push Back." The New York Times, 9 May 2005.

"College Entrance Exam." Korea4expats website.

Koo, Se-woong. "An Assault Upon Our Children." The New York Times, The New York Times, 1 Aug. 2014.

Sharif, Hossein. "Suneung: The Day Silence Falls Over South Korea." BBC News, 26 Nov. 2018.

24 I'm Not Surprised at the College Admissions Scandal, and You Shouldn't Be Either

by Maria Olifer, 18 (2019)

The lunchroom was louder than usual as seniors read the news on their phones. Twenty-five million dollars? Perfect scores fabricated by an agency? Photoshopped athletes? No wonder I couldn't get in!

The college admissions scandal erupted on March 12, 2019, as United States federal prosecutors brought to light a conspiracy to influence student admissions into prominent U.S. universities. Wealthy families would pay the Key Worldwide Foundation or The Edge College & Career Network—foundations led by William Rick Singer—which would then use this money to bribe test proctors to take standardized tests for the students; coaches at Ivy League institutions to assure the admissions officers that said student is a world-class tennis player despite the fact that they have never picked up a racket; or any number of other avenues to acceptance that could be paved with the power of the American dollar.

The frightening reality isn't that students are being admitted based on their parents' wealth; it's that the general populace is shocked by this.

This year, I applied to 11 universities. Each university had an application fee averaging $80. I had to pay to take the ACT ($62 per attempt, 2 attempts) and the Advanced Placement (AP) exam ($94 per exam, 13 exams); for each prep book that I used to study; and then again to send these scores to colleges. This means that I spent about $2,500 on applications alone, and while my family could pay, the cost was noticeable.

However, not everyone is as lucky. To be a competitive candidate for top schools, students are expected to not only maintain good grades and have good test scores, but to have multiple leadership opportunities, play sports, and partake in internships in their spare time. If your weekend job is integral to your family paying rent on time, these résumé fillers become difficult to achieve.

The college admissions scandal should not serve as another reason to detest the ultra-wealthy, but rather as a platform for education reform. Going to college in America requires approximately 53 percent of parents' salary in the face of a constant rise in tuition and stagnant wages; whereas in Europe, high taxes—anywhere from 37 to 56 percent income tax, paid over the course of a lifetime—result in the opportunity for "free" college for a majority of those who seek it. The reality is that college will never be completely free, but there need to be more plans in place to decrease the cost. While the Federal Pell Grant only covers tuition, applying it to encompass a wider socio-economic bracket would be less contentious than raising taxes on the public and would result in more instantaneous impact. It would be a start.

Sources

Brinded, Lianna. "10 of the Most Expensive Countries for a University Education." Independent, 28 Dec. 2015.

Harris, Adam. "The College-Affordability Crisis Is Uniting the 2020 Democratic Candidates." The Atlantic, 26 Feb. 2019.

Jackson, Abby. " 'Free' College in Europe Isn't Really Free." Business Insider, 25 Jun. 2015.

Levitz, Jennifer, and Melissa Korn. "Two Parents in College-Admissions Scheme Indicted on New Charge." The Wall Street Journal, 26 Mar. 2019.

Lombardo, Clare. "How Admissions Really Work: If the College Admissions Scandal Shocked You, Read This." NPR, 23 Mar. 2019.

Taylor, Kate. "12 People, Including 6 Coaches, Plead Not Guilty in College Admissions Scandal." The New York Times, 25 Mar. 2019.

25 Cutting it Short

by Eric Vogt (2014)

The common view among high school students is that a shorter assignment is an easier one, a view that is, in part, propagated by the stereotype of the "traditional" high school writing assignment. This is precisely why a student is taken by surprise when her teachers asks that she write not at least 450 words, but at most 450 words. For the first time, the student is faced with a maximum. A limit. Gone is the need to type in 13-point font and subtly narrow the margins, hoping that the teacher will not notice. With a sigh of relief, the student will return home, and wait until the night before the short-form writing assignment is due to sit down and begin typing it. That student has made a tragic mistake, and will not be getting much sleep. The student is not to blame, as her school system has failed to introduce her to the short form.

Short writing assignments are uniquely challenging in that they require a student to not only say something, but do so as efficiently as possible. Traditional essays only ask a student to present an argument, without any sort of regard for word count. Establishing both a sense of reliability and a solid argument in a couple sentences is an art, for which current high school students are not prepared. "When you have only a sentence or two, there's nowhere to hide," explains Andy Selsberg, English teacher at John Jay College, a man who sees the ideal writing assignment to be the length of the common text message.

Traditional writing is not without its supporters. Often seen as more artistic and in-depth than something the length of a text message, extended writing will no doubt be defended by those who thumb their noses at risk-takers like Selsberg. What these naysayers fail to recognize is that the world is kicking lengthy forms of communication to the curb. A standard text message has only 160 characters. A tweet holds a paltry 140. These short messages are frequently being used to carry vital communications, deciding everything from dinner to the fate of a relationship. “It wasn’t the volume of messages but their content that affected the quality of relationships,” says Alexandra Sifferlin, reporting the results of a study conducted on couples and text messages. The study conclusively showed that lengthening an explanation did not improve it. Quality trumps quantity.

The steps towards the future are clear. Teaching efficiency will allow students to take full advantage of modern communication. Without wasting any breath, high schools must turn their primary focus towards the short form, and knock the traditional essay from its long-held dominance.

Sources

Selsberg, Andy. “Teaching to the Text Message.” The New York Times, 19 March 2011.

Sifferlin, Alexandra. “Textual Relations.” Time.com, 31 Oct. 2013.

26 Fairness in Education: The Upper-Class Monopoly on Resources

by Xiaolin Ding, 17 (2018)

Education has become an industry in which the upper-class's monopoly of resources is unchecked. A New York Times study of 38 top colleges in America, including five Ivy League schools, found that more students came from the top 1 percent of the income scale than from the entire bottom 60 percent. China faces a similar conundrum, where rich families in urban areas can send their kids to "keypoint" high schools. These schools receive more funding per student than average schools, have better teachers, and reliably place their students into elite colleges. In a world where income inequality is growing—China's bottom 25 percent owns less than 1 percent of the aggregate wealth while the top 1 percent owns over one-third—one wonders if people not born into wealth are doomed to poverty.

However, in 2016, the Chinese Ministry of Education sparked hope when it announced 140,000 spaces—about 6.5 percent of spots in top colleges—would be reserved for students from less developed provinces. Unfortunately, this policy immediately ignited strong protests by urban parents. Under protest banners of "fairness in education," protesters rallied to preserve using "Gaokao" college-entrance examination score, as the sole metric. They noted that Gaokao mimics China's old imperial civil service exam ("Keju") in relying purely on exam results and praised this meritocratic system as superior. Essentially, their argument is that in the long race of college applications, no one should be forced to run 6.5 percent further than their competitors.

What these protesters failed to mention is that times have changed, and the race's participants begin on vastly different starting lines. The Keju system that was effective in bringing people from rural areas to government posts in cities, and thus increased social mobility, is not applicable in a country experiencing the fastest urbanization trend in history. As recently as 1993, over 40 percent of students in China's colleges were children of farmers or factory workers. But now social mobility is becoming an obsolete concept. Today, less than 10 percent of young people in the countryside go to senior high schools compared with 70 percent of their urban counterparts.

Fairness in education is the right slogan, but a truly meritocratic system should not ignore complex social realities that put some students at a disadvantage from a young age. The Chinese government's new higher-education admissions policy is a step toward balancing the unequal 'starting lines' that poor, rural students face. More such creative, comprehensive policies should be encouraged. Without these measures, growing inequality in society cannot be redressed. Every citizen—regardless of location, family background or wealth—should have hope that hard work and dedication can transform their lives.

Sources

Aisch, Gregor, et al. "Some Colleges Have More Students From the Top 1 Percent Than the Bottom 60. Find Yours." The New York Times, 18 Jan. 2017.

"China's Dirty Little Secret: Its Growing Wealth Gap." Economy, South China Morning Post, 13 July 2017.

Hernández, Javier C. "China Tries to Redistribute Education to the Poor, Igniting Class Conflict." The New York Times, 11 June 2016.

"The Class Ceiling." The Economist, The Economist Group Limited, 4 June 2016.

27 Inferior Substitute Teaching

by Candice C. and Cheryl B. (2014)

"Gabriel?"

Here.

"Joe?"

Here.

"Madilyn Mesa?"

Here.

"Sarah-with-an-H? Absent? Okay, Sarah-with-an-H is absent today."

And that was all we got out of our A.P. Language sub for the day. As soon as roll call was over, he headed back to the teacher's desk and hid behind the computer, leaving us to figure out what to do for the rest of the period. What essential duty had called him away from the class of 35 advanced students? Spider Solitaire, of course.

This situation—one where students essentially teach themselves when a substitute is called in—is identical for thousands of high school kids around the country each day. The problem is not always laziness but ranges from incompetence to lack of subject knowledge. Yes, not all substitute teachers resemble the one described above. Yes, high school students may be difficult to work with. Yes, it is difficult to come into a classroom and teach an unfamiliar subject. But this national trend of untrained, inactive, subpar substitute teachers must come to an end for the sake of our nation's scholars.

Substitute teachers, however, are the symptoms of deeper problems within education, not the source. Lax hiring techniques, little to no training, and low expectations are just the tip of the iceberg when it comes to obstacles faced by subs. According to the Times article "The Replacements," 77 percent of American school districts give substitute teachers no training, 56 percent of districts hire subs without conducting face-to-face interviews, and not a single state requires that substitutes hold a teaching degree. This problem can also be reflected by the fact that an average of 9 percent of teachers nationwide are absent every day, adding up to approximately one year that students have with substitutes by the time they graduate from high school. If this problem is not solved, students will be the ones to suffer the consequences of an inadequate education.

So what can we do? What can we, concerned parents, teachers, and students, do to make sure that a school day with a substitute does not become a waste? We can make sure that subs are adequately trained before being allowed to shape the minds of America's future leaders. We can have teachers evaluate their experiences with substitutes. We can institute higher standards for hiring subs, along with higher pay. And most importantly, we can make sure substitute teachers are comfortable with the subjects and class levels that they teach. With so many options to act upon, it would be a crime for students to suffer one more "free period" of inferior substitute teaching.

Sources

Bucior, Carolyn. "The Replacements." The New York Times. 2 Jan. 2010.

Dyer, John. "Some school systems outsourcing search for substitute teachers." Boston Globe. 6 Feb., 2014.

28 Why We Stayed Up Until Midnight Finishing This Editorial

by Jean Z., Sarah X., and Gjeorgjinio B. (2014)

"There are four pillars to a successful high school career," said this college counselor. "Academics, athletics, extracurriculars, and volunteering. My secret is for my client to start something. It could just be a small non-profit, but it really shows leadership skills and makes your college application stand out." It was the summer of seventh grade and my parents were taking me to talk to college advisers.

Parents and teachers push this cruel false reality that our whole life depends on the four years of high school as a teenager. Teenagers have this constant pressure from their environment to do better and more at one of the most vulnerable times in their lives. It is taught that going to a good college leads to a good job and a good life. Clearly, it isn't that simple.

A high-achieving student with a sport, extracurricular, and four honors or AP classes is usually done with his or her homework past midnight. This doesn't include a social life, or even dinner. But after hours of work, training, and volunteering, these students are exactly the same as the thousands of other students aiming for the same highly selective colleges.

According to psychologist Robert Leahy, the average high schooler today has the same level of anxiety as the average psychiatric patient in the early 1950s. As Alfie Kohn from The New York Times said, "Gambling their [children's] mental health and love of learning in the hopes of acceptance at an extremely selective college is a bet that no caring, rational parent should take." The American Psychological Association found that 45% of all teens said they were stressed by school pressures. This stress can cause mental issues including anxiety, depression, and social withdrawal.

School stress also hurts the physical health of students. A National Sleep Foundation poll found that only 20% of teenagers report getting the recommended amount of sleep. Lack of sleep and school stress have physical effects, including headaches, chest pain, and low energy. High-achieving students are unable to handle the high levels of school stress without physical and mental repercussions.

The solution to this growing problem is to change the educational practices that support the stigma that success is your college application. A student should be taught to only take as much work and pressure as they can handle. Educators and parents need to change the attitudes and policies that cause these overwhelming school pressures.

It isn't right to tell the students with five hours of homework to take a few deep breaths. We should not be desperately trying to handle the stress of this system. We should be changing the system itself.

Sources

Clark, Taylor. "It's Not the Job Market." Slate. 31 Jan. 2011.

Kohn, Alfie. "Reconsider Attitudes About Success." The New York Times, 12 Dec., 2010.

Neighmond, Patti. "School Stress Takes A Toll On Health, Teens And Parents Say." National Public Radio. 2 Dec. 2013.

"Sleep in America Poll." National Sleep Foundation. (2006) PDF file.

"Stress Symptoms." Web MD.

29 We Need Music in Our Schools

by Gabe M., 13 (2016)

I love music. I love listening to music, I love playing music, and I love writing music. Sadly, ever since fifth grade, I have had to get all my music playing and writing outside of school: My school doesn't provide any music training after fourth grade. My school and all other schools without music programs should try their best to add music education to the curriculum for all ages, not just elementary school students.

Research shows that music education boosts students' academic success. One study found that when schools with different music programs were compared, on average, the schools with superior music programs score 20 percent higher on standardized English tests and 22 percent higher on standardized math tests, regardless of socioeconomic status. Another study showed that when one group of children were given piano training, "the group scored 27 percent higher on proportional math and fractions tests" then the group that did not have piano training (Rauscher et al.). This is because music is full of math. Even when students aren't consciously thinking about the math behind the music, they're constantly exercising mathematical thinking while playing music, from logarithmic scales on a guitar fretboard to fraction multiplication in a drumming polyrhythm. Take it from Pythagoras: "There is geometry in the humming of the strings, there is music in the spacing of the spheres." An analysis of U.S. Department of Education data found that "Students who report consistent high levels of involvement in instrumental music over the middle and high school years show significantly higher levels of mathematics proficiency by grade 12." (Catterall, Chapleau, and Iwanaga).

But music's benefits extend beyond school; teens busy playing music are less likely to get involved with drugs or gang violence. Teens also learn good work habits from practicing an instrument and collaboration from playing in ensembles. In the words of Lois Hetland and Ellen Winner of

Project Zero according to The New York Times, "Students who study the arts seriously are taught to see better, to envision, to persist, to be playful and learn from mistakes, to make critical judgments and justify such judgments." Lastly, music is an enormous part of our culture. Music training is crucial to growth of adolescents.

Despite these advantages, increasing funding for music (or any program) in a public school is easier said than done. However, I do believe that parents, teachers, school administrators and voters should do their best to put music in our schools. As Plato once said, "I would teach children music, physics and philosophy; but most importantly music, for the patterns in music and all the arts are the keys to learning."

Sources

Catterall, James S., Richard Chapleau, and John Iwanaga. "Involvement in the Arts and Human Development: General Involvement and Intensive Involvement In Music and Theater Arts." Rep. N.p.: n.p., 1999. Web. 26 Mar. 2016.

Graziano, A.B., M. Peterson, and G.L. Shaw. "Enhanced Learning of Proportional Math through Music Training and Spatial Temporal Reasoning." Neurological Research 21.2 (1999): 139-52. PubMed. Web. 26 Mar. 2016.

Johnson, Christopher M., and Jenny E. Memmott. "Examination of Relationships between Participation in School Music Programs of Differing Quality and Standardized Test Results." Journal of Research in Music Education 54.4 (2006): 293. Web. 26 Mar. 2016.

Pogrebin, Robin. "Book Tackles Old Debate: Role of Art in Schools." The New York Times. The New York Times, 03 Aug. 2007. Web. 26 Mar. 2016.

Civic Life and Politics

"The same people thought of as too immature to vote started a worldwide movement against gun violence."

"My crime? The American passport that I carry says that I was born in Iraq."

"I am one of those 175,000 abandoned children who ended up in an orphanage."

30 Dinner Table Politics

by Bridget Smith, 15 (2018)

The Thanksgiving table is a war zone. The soldiers? The conservative aunt who drove all the way from Alabama. The ultra-progressive sibling who makes passive-aggressive comments while passing the potatoes. And, of course the grandparents, who stubbornly reference the good ol' days when political incorrectness roamed free. Throughout America, families hunker down for the holidays with reluctance and trepidation. Civil conversation concerning the issues facing our country is becoming rarer by the day. But if we can't talk about the issues, how can we fix them? The Thanksgiving table is a microcosm of the real world discussions in local and state governments, in Washington, in the White House itself. Americans must learn how to talk to each other about politics, from the dinner table to the Oval Office.

I've had my fair share of political discourse with friends and family. These conversations escalate quickly and infuriate easily, but haven't destroyed my relationships. I listen, disagree and discuss. However, when faced with opposing viewpoints, many Americans polarize further. Instead of talking to those with whom they disagree, Americans find like-minded individuals who cater to their political tastes. In fact, according to The New York Times, "Liberals and Conservatives prefer to associate and live near their fellow partisans," and "would be unhappy if their children married someone with a different political viewpoint." This is troubling. We develop empathy when we talk with people from different backgrounds who challenge our beliefs.

Our lack of conversation has turned us into our rigid, stubborn grandparents unwilling to consider alternative views. According to Pew Research, 38 percent of Democrats have consistently liberal views, a dramatic increase from 1994 when only 8 percent remained consistently liberal. America's lack of political plasticity is growing rapidly, creating a chasm between the things we support and the things we don't. We see this divide every year at the Thanksgiving table. If we can't set aside what we think we know and talk to our stubborn grandparents, we become our stubborn grandparents. We remain entrenched and the gravy gets cold.

Talking to people we disagree with is hard. But it should be easier to disagree with the people we love. Talking to family is a starting point to bridge that political chasm. Ask your aunt why she feels that way. Ask your grandparents what shapes their beliefs. Ask your siblings to suggest solutions. If we can empathize with our family at the Thanksgiving table, we can empathize with our neighbors, friends and political representatives. Don't let your dinner table become a war zone. Talk to your fellow Americans. Ask them questions. Invite them to dinner. And most importantly, show up and speak your mind. You might start a new tradition.

Sources

Cohn, Nate. "Polarization Is Dividing American Society, Not Just Politics." The New York Times, 12 June 2014.

"Political Polarization in the American Public." Pew Research, 12 June 2014.

31 Civil Obedience

by Anushka Agarwal, 16 (2018)

When I was five, I needed someone to hold my hand as I entered school. When I was twelve, I needed someone to point to the entrance, but I could walk in alone. Now, at sixteen, I don't need anyone—I'm a different person: independent and mature. Yet, I am treated as if I'm still a child.

After the horrific Florida shooting, students walked out of their classes in honor of the 17 lives lost. As noted in "How Young is Too Young for Protest? A National Gun Violence Protest Tests Schools," even Utah's Wood Cross Elementary School staged a protest in the school gym to allow the students to experience "a little civil disobedience."

Like Wood Cross, the administration at my school staged our protest. The day before the walkout, a minute-by-minute schedule and list of guidelines—including the only two doors we could exit from—were uploaded onto Facebook. The next day, our obedient student body shuffled into the fenced area between our school buildings only to witness teachers' comments about how "cute" we were and their apologies for being 60 seconds behind schedule. By 10:05, the end of the designated "shouting time," my friends and I lowered our posters in defeat.

Although I am thankful that my school supports the walkout, nobody needed to be hand-held through this protest. Protesting is fighting and risking consequences, risking falling. Protesting is true civil disobedience. Yet Henry David Thoreau is rolling in his grave thinking about our "protest." In "Civil Disobedience," Thoreau does not "lend [himself] to the wrong which [he condemns]." Instead, he fights against it, because he has the right "to do at any time what [he thinks is] right." We have the same right. Why prevent us from using it?

Maybe the elementary schoolers play along, but I cannot. We already have mock organizations: mock trial, model U.N., and now this walkout. The school coddles us. Highlighted in a New York Times article, the students who excelled after high school were the ones who fell and got up afterward. But if schools are going to cushion each one of our falls, how will we grow up?

I understand schools' concern: safety first. Parents may be uncomfortable with their children protesting. But the goal of civil disobedience is to make others uncomfortable. Discomfort brings change. Change from our parents' generation to ours.

We need adults to accept the discomfort of us taking the reins of the gun violence movement and growing up. Otherwise, if fearful adults keep holding us back, how can we grow up to become fearless leaders?

Sources

Saul, Stephanie, and Anemona Hartocollis. "How Young Is Too Young for Protest? A National Gun-Violence Walkout Tests Schools." The New York Times, 13 March 2018.

Thoreau, Henry David, 1817-1862. Civil Disobedience: Complete Texts With Introduction, Historical Contexts, Critical Essays. Boston: Houghton Mifflin, 2000. Print.

Tough, Paul. "What If the Secret to Success Is Failure?" The New York Times, 14 Sept. 2011.

32 Generation Code Red

by Grace Scullion, 16 (2017)

One day after school, I ran into the kitchen and saw the breaking news crack my sturdy mother. Her skin turned paler with each name listed on the television. This time it was a group of first graders from Sandy Hook. Standing in the kitchen with my backpack by my feet, I could not escape the visions of carnage.

In school, we practice Code Red. We pile furniture against classroom doors and sit silently, holding our breath until reminded that it is just a drill. Wariness follows me home from school, its tentacles twisting my head.

When I pick up my phone, there are notifications reading, "At least 50 dead after nightclub shooting in Orlando, officials report" next to Snapchat notifications. I can list Adam Lanza, Dylann Roof, Omar Mateen, Robert Dear and Chris Harper-Mercer, just as quickly as I can list the names of my best friends.

I notice that when the bullets hit the kids, our civilized side flares. But we build the excuses back up, brick by brick, into cities and laws and Second Amendments. I am mad because 16-year-olds are supposed to be angry with their parents and society and not having a date to the prom, but instead I have to be angry with lawmakers and the N.R.A. and an entire country that lets holsters and bazookas pull its puppet strings. I can fire off facts faster than an AR-15 rifle: last year, there were 358 shootings in the U.S. in which four or more people were injured or killed. 306 Americans are shot every day. 48 of those are children or teenagers.

It does not have to be this way. Take Australia. After a shooting in 1996 left 35 civilians dead, extensive gun control legislature was passed. These new laws included required licenses, safety training courses and an assault weapons ban. In the twenty years since the legislature was passed, there have been no mass shootings in Australia. This is sensible action. This is making sure guns do not end up in the wrong hands.

Dear lawmakers: I challenge you to think about the American people. Think about the 306 Americans who will feel bullets tearing into their skin tomorrow. Think about the American students holding their breath in the corners of dark classrooms.

Sources

Kauffman, Gretel. "Why Australia Isn't a Model for US Gun Control." The Christian Science Monitor. The Christian Science Monitor, 23 June 2016. Web. 4 Apr. 2017.

"Key Gun Violence Statistics." Brady Campaign to Prevent Gun Violence. Brady Campaign to Prevent Gun Violence, n.d. Web. 04 Apr. 2017.

Quealy, Kevin, and Margot Sanger-Katz. "Compare These Gun Death Rates: The U.S. Is in a Different World." The New York Times. The New York Times, 13 June 2016. Web. 4 Apr. 2017.

33 Lessons for 2020 Democratic Presidential Candidates, From a Soon-to-be First-Time Voter

by Nora Fellas, 17 (2019)

I am one of more than five million people too young to vote today, but who will be old enough in 2020. I am 16, I run a political blog with over 100,000 followers, and I am offering some free lessons to candidates on how they can earn our votes.

Given the slim margin in the 2016 election, our votes could make all the difference. So listen up.

While young people have diverse views, Democrats focus on issues that matter to many of us, like gun control and climate change, making them more attractive than the presumptive Republican nominee, President Trump. The challenge for Democratic candidates is to distinguish themselves to capture the youth vote.

So what actually matters to us? It's simple, but elusive: authenticity.

When politicians force relatability, they seem fake. Prior to her bid, Elizabeth Warren Instagram livestreamed and began by announcing to the camera, "I'm gonna get me a beer," and then thanked her husband for being there, in their own house, as if it hadn't all been scripted. One Boston Herald analyst criticized the image of the "multi-million-dollar Cambridge law professor poppin' a brewski." It's not credible that Warren opened Instagram and decided to livestream of her own volition.

In 2016, Secretary Clinton and Trump both tried to appeal to young people. Trump used Twitter, and his statements were so unfiltered that they could only have come from him. Clinton's messaging, however, felt phony. In a particularly cringey video, Clinton said, "Pokemon Go to the polls," referencing the tween-trending app of that summer, Pokemon Go. It was clear that she had been fed that line and it felt condescending, suggesting youth votes could be earned by name-dropping a game.

This isn't to say candidates shouldn't appeal to young people—they must, because our votes can't be taken for granted. In 2016, 18-29 year olds had the lowest turnout of any age group. The key difference between our generation and our parents' is that we belong to the "Bernie or Bust" generation. 2016 revealed that we won't choose between "the lesser of two evils"; if no candidate inspires us, we will just stay home.

This is why politicians need to appeal seriously to youth voters. Take Sanders: he is nearly 80, yet he is incredibly popular among young people. Why? Not because of his Instagram skills, but because he's perceived as genuine—his politics haven't changed.

To the 2020 candidates: the key to earning our vote isn't pandering to us. Rather, we want to see that you genuinely care about the issues that matter to us. If you do that, you won't need to worry about spreading your message on Instagram. We'll do it for you.

Sources

"Clinton Drops a Pokemon Go Reference at Rally." YouTube, uploaded by CNN, 14 July 2016.

"Elizabeth Warren Drinking a Beer on Instagram Live Gets Mixed Reactions." YouTube, uploaded by CBS News, 2 Jan. 2019.

Ember, Sydney. "Bernie Sanders Begins 2020 Race With Some Familiar Themes and a New One: Himself." The New York Times, 2 March 2019.

Fellas, Nora (@nastyfeminism). Instagram.

Graham, Michael. "Elizabeth Warren Pours a Cold One—on Image of Authenticity." Boston Herald, 4 Jan. 2019.

Khalid, Asma. "Millennials Now Rival Boomers As A Political Force, But Will They Actually Vote?" NPR, 16 May 2016.

Martin, Joyce A., Brady E. Hamilton, Paul D. Sutton, Stephanie J. Ventura, Fay Menacker, and Martha L. Munson. "Births: Final Data for 2002." National Vital Statistics Report, Centers for Disease Control and Prevention, 17 Dec. 2003.

34 In Nothing We Trust

by Francesca Kelley, 18 (2017)

Like many American children, I have, at one point or another, dabbled in door-to-door sales. I eventually graduated from peddling Girl Scout cookies with my mom to knocking on my neighbors' doors alone, attempting to lure them into supporting my high school marching band with citrus fruits. However, selling alone, I soon encountered a problem: I knew almost none of them by name. Additionally, even after explaining that I lived just down the block, I often noticed the homeowner eyeing me with suspicion, questioning what business I could possibly have on their front porch.

Gone are the halcyon days of perpetually unlocked doors and packs of unsupervised kids roving the neighborhood. America has entered a new era: the Age of Mistrust.

Nowadays, suburban homes are outfitted with security systems fit for federal penitentiaries, and children aren't allowed out of the house without a chaperone. It is no coincidence that as we have lost trust in those around us, loneliness levels have also been on the rise; whereas between 11 and 20 percent of people frequently felt lonely in the 1970s and 80s, that number is closer to 40 percent today.

Unfortunately, the disease of mistrust hasn't just been eroding our happiness. The American public is also rapidly losing faith in its most valued institutions. Today, in the country that once considered the newsman Walter Cronkite "the most trusted man in America," only 32 percent of people have a "great deal" or "fair amount" of trust in the media. According to the Pew Research Center, an abysmal 19 percent of Americans trust their government. So where did all our trust go, and how do we get it back?

In a bygone America, neighbors relied on each other to watch the kids or borrow some sugar. The moment we started locking our doors was the moment we began to lose faith in what once made our country great. Social scientists have noticed the steady decline in interpersonal trust has led to an inability "to engage in spontaneous, voluntary cooperation." What it boils down to is this: when someone can't even trust their neighbor, how can they trust their president, or a refugee from a foreign land?

As bleak as the situation may seem, we can learn to trust again. Communities across America demonstrate the possibilities every day, whether by rallying around a local child fighting cancer, or organizing a fund-raiser to help feed the homeless. Trust is key; a community can't unite for the common good without believing in each other.

America has lost its way, but the solution is simple: love thy neighbor.

Sources

Elving, Ron. "Poll: 1 In 5 Americans Trusts The Government." NPR. NPR, 23 Nov. 2015. Web. 21 Mar. 2017.

Entis, Lauren. "Chronic Loneliness Is a Modern-Day Epidemic." Fortune. 22 June 2016. Web. 21 Mar. 2017.

Heath, Joseph. "Is Trust Still Possible in the U.S.?" The New York Times. The New York Times, 08 Nov. 2016. Web. 21 Mar. 2017.

Levine, Cecilia. "Community Rallies For Fair Lawn Girl, Cousin Both Fighting Cancer." Fair Lawn-Glen Rock Daily Voice. 01 Apr. 2017. Web. 03 Apr. 2017.

Slade, Shelby. "Bowls for Humanity Rallies Community, Artists around Helping Homeless." Daily Herald. 01 Apr. 2017. Web. 03 Apr. 2017.

Walsh, Kenneth T. "Distrust of Media at Highest Level Ever." US News. 15 Sept. 2016. Web. 21 Mar. 2017.

35 China, It's Time to Meet Your Daughters

by Lila McNamee, 14 (2019)

In 1979, China implemented a one-child policy to solve its overpopulation problem. This policy created a dilemma for families, particularly given the cultural preference for male children. It is estimated that the one-child policy prevented the births of 400 million children, and forced thousands more, primarily girls, to be abandoned. I am one of those 175,000 abandoned children who ended up in an orphanage, ultimately adopted to be raised in America.

In 2015, China relaxed its policy, allowing two children per family. This was not due to the realization by the central government that the policy was immoral, but rather because they needed to protect their future. The one-child policy had created a number of unforeseen problems for China. For example, the distinct preference for boys had led to gender imbalance, and by 2050, there will be a major labor shortage due to the aging population.

China has attempted to address these statistical problems, but it is time that the government concentrates on the effect this policy had on its people, and what they can do about it. It's time they focus on the personal, not the political. The human rights of the parents and children were denied for over 35 years. Some people have said that I'm lucky to be in America and that I have a better life here, but is that really true? Yes, I go to an amazing school, have an incredible mother, and love living in Los Angeles. However, I don't know my genetic makeup, the time I was born, and don't get to know my biological family. The Chinese government took my identity from me. I have always just been Asian. . . . dark straight hair, brown almond eyes, good at math. I have never experienced the "lunch-box moment," and just recently learned what the "Asian squat" is (and I'm pretty sure I do it wrong). Although I take Mandarin and feel connected to Chinese culture, I wish I knew more about me. What is my family medical history? Do I have siblings? Who do I look like?

The Chinese government took these things from me and 175,000 others. It's time they try to make amends. I don't want a generic letter saying, "We're sorry." I want a letter with my genetic information. The government could set up a program where families could submit their DNA, the approximate birth date of their child, and their province/district, giving Chinese adoptees a real chance to find the parents that were forced to give them away. I dream of meeting my biological family, and I think the Chinese government owes me the opportunity to make that happen.

Sources

Clarke, Aileen. "See How the One-Child Policy Changed China." National Geographic, 13 Nov. 2015.

Clemetson, Lynette. "Adopted in China, Seeking Identity in America." The New York Times, 23 Mar. 2006.

Lee, Jenni Fang. "A Letter of Frustration and Gratitude on the End of China's One-Child Policy." Huffington Post, 30 Oct. 2015.

"Somewhere Between." Directed by Linda Goldstein Knowlton. Long Shot Factory and Ladylike Films, 2011.

36 That's Not My Problem: The Bystander Effect in Today's Society

by Cassidy Remboski, 17 (2019)

On a frigid night in the midst of Michigan's polar vortex, I found myself stranded in a grocery store parking lot with an unchangeable flat tire. I was clearly in need of assistance; I was crying and my coat and face were riddled with dried blood splotches from a cut on my finger. Despite this, I was met only with sideways glances from over thirty individuals who likely assumed that someone else was going to help me.

We've all been in a situation where we feel compelled to help someone, but something is holding us back. This is called the bystander effect, a phenomenon when we push the responsibility of helping someone onto those around us. A study conducted by John Darley and Bibb Latane in 1968 revealed that while 85 percent of people would respond to someone in need, that number dropped dramatically to 31 percent when they thought four or more people around them also saw the individual (Darley). And in my case, that number dropped to zero.

In short, the more people who are present, the less likely we are to help.

So why is it that we neglect those in need because of others being around? Are we afraid of judgements? If this were true wouldn't others view us more positively for doing a good deed in the public eye? Are we simply conforming to the inaction of others (Cherry)? If so, why are we trusting their judgements over our own?

Long-term data collected by the General Social Survey dating back to 1972 has revealed that Americans trust each other far less than in the past 40 years; making them evermore hesitant to help even their fellow citizens when in distress (Ortiz-Ospina).

But that leaves those in honest need of aid stranded.

Maybe in that grocery store I didn't clearly vocalize for help, but maybe

I was in a place where I couldn't ask due to emotional or physical limitation either.

When we judge books by their covers we neglect the facts behind someone's situation.

As Joe Nocera wrote in his editorial "It's Hard to Be a Hero" after analyzing the bystander effect, "We don't really know how we'd act until the moment is upon us. Sadly, science says we're more likely to do nothing than respond . . ." (Nocera).

This statement holds true in today's society, but maybe it's time to break this cycle of pushing responsibility on others and take it upon ourselves. So next time you see someone in need of assistance, instead of assuming they can handle it or someone else will help, assume that nobody is going to help but you—and maybe in the future when *you* need help someone will do the same.

Sources

Cherry, Kendra. "Understanding the Bystander Effect." Verywell Mind, 27 Dec. 2018.

Darley, John M., and Bibb Latane. "Bystander Intervention in Emergencies: Diffusion of Responsibility." Journal of Personality and Social Psychology, vol. 8, no. 4, 1968, pp. 378–379.

Nocera, Joe. "It's Hard to Be a Hero." The New York Times, 7 Dec. 2012.

Ortiz-Ospina, Esteban, and Max Roser. "Trust." Our World in Data, 22 July 2016.

37 It's Time for Teens to Vote

by Miriam Gold, 14 (2016)

At sixteen years old, Jack Andraka discovered an inexpensive method to test for pancreatic cancer. At just fifteen, Louis Braille invented the Braille writing system, allowing the blind to read and write. Additionally, Malala Yousafzai was seventeen when she won the Nobel Peace Prize for promoting women's education in Pakistan. These teens show themselves to be innovators and inspirers, their work rivaling the achievements of our most celebrated adults. However, even with the potential that every teen holds, they are denied a voice in who governs their own country. As a politically aware high school student, I should be allowed to vote at sixteen in the November 2016 election because my opinion is no less valid than the adults who vote.

Throughout history, restricted voting has been a way for the government to stifle the voices of those they did not want to hear. In 1870, blacks were finally given the right to vote; and in 1920, Congress gave voting rights to women. Finally, Americans understood that no matter what group someone belonged to, their right to vote should be protected—except one group, teens. Through unfair voting law, teens are told that the fundamental rights of all Americans do not apply to them.

Many who deny teens' rights to vote believe teens will make uninformed decisions that will hurt the country. Although many teens may seem not to care about voting now, this could easily be changed. An extremely effective ways to increase voting interest is "to inoculate [teens] with a significant dose of meaningful responsibility and authority" (Epstein 17). If students are given the responsibility of a vote that will affect their life, most will become more invested in electing the best candidate.

Although teens are not extended the rights of adults, they are still burdened with the responsibilities. In many states, "A child, defined as a person under age 18, can be tried as an adult if the child was age 14 or older at the time of the offense" ("How"). If our society believes teens can handle the burden of adult responsibility, why are they believed undeserving of adult rights?

Not only do teens deserve the right to vote, their votes would prove constructive to society. Research shows political involvement by teens to "trickle up" to their parents, increasing voter turnout, and, "Empirical evidence suggests that the earlier in life a voter casts their first ballot, the more likely they are to develop voting as a habit" ("Lower"). Low voter turnout is only worsening, but teen voting could help turn this issue around because countless teenagers like myself would be proud to fill out the ballots deciding our country's future.

Sources

Belluck, Pam. "Sixteen Candles, but Few Blazing a Trail to the Ballot Box." The New York Times. The New York Times, 26 Aug. 2007. Web. 24 Mar. 2016.

"Chapter 12. Political Socialization and Civic Competence." Political Attitudes and Democracy in Five Nations The Civic Culture (2006): n. pag. Web. 24 Mar. 2016.

Epstein, Robert. Teen 2.0: Saving Our Children and Families From the Torment of Adolescence. Fresno, CA: Quill Driver/Word Dancer, 2010. Print.

Giacomo, Carol. "A Nobel Peace Prize for Malala Yousafzai." The New York Times n.d.: n. pag. Taking Note: A Nobel Peace Prize for Malala Yousafzai Comments. The New York Times, 10 Oct. 2014. Web. 24 Mar. 2016.

"How Are Juveniles Tried as Adults?" Ohio State Bar Association. www.ohiobar.org, 21 Sept. 2015. Web. 24 Mar. 2016.

Kaiman, Jonathan, Amanda Holpuch, David Smith, Jonathan Watts and Alexandra Topping. "Beyond Malala: Six Teenagers Changing the World." The Guardian. Guardian News and Media, 18 Oct. 2013. Web. 24 Mar. 2016.

"Lower the Voting Age—FairVote." FairVote. N.p., n.d. Web. 24 Mar. 2016.

"Why October Is Youth History Month." Youth History Month. Pro-Youth Pages, 2007. Web. 24 Mar. 2016.

38 The Case for Lowering the Voting Age

by Kathryn Zaia, 14 (2018)

Only a freshman in high school myself, until recently I had always accepted the idea that teenagers lack all responsibility. Convinced that high schoolers possessed insufficient maturity to vote, I dismissed the idea as absurd.

I was all the more shocked after attending the "March for Our Lives" on March 24th. Organized by high school students, the strength and courage that all the young speakers possessed were truly inspiring. My awe was shared by all who attended the march. The event finally reversed my doubt in my fellow teenagers. If high school students can organize a worldwide march in the face of an issue as difficult as gun violence, they are more than capable of voting. The time has come to lower the voting age to sixteen.

For those who doubt a younger person's commitment to voting, consider the example of Takoma Park, Maryland. This suburb of Washington has permitted 16- and 17-year-olds to vote in local elections. The first election drew registered people in this age group at over four times the rate of older registered voters. Why hesitate to include a new demographic of voters, more eager and engaged even than their older counterparts?

Not only are younger people eager and willing to vote, but they are ready for the responsibility. By many standards, the age of sixteen is the beginning of adulthood. It is the age of responsibility, a time when maturity becomes an expectation. A common argument against lowering the voting age is that younger voters are incapable of making a well-advised decision. Yet at the same time, sixteen-year-olds are given the right to drive. It seems clear that anyone trusted with sound enough decision-making to protect the lives of those they share the road with should be trusted with their own vote.

Beyond being trusted with others' lives, younger people are expected to shape their own. As a high school student, I can tell you of the constant emphasis on colleges and grade point averages, perpetual talk of how every one of our actions will shape the rest of our lives. By the time we turn sixteen, shouldn't we be permitted to vote and given true power to shape our futures?

It is high time to challenge the perception of teenagers as entirely incompetent and irresponsible. The same people thought of as too immature to vote started a worldwide movement against gun violence. Not only does this show capability and political awareness, but proof that younger people deserve to have their voices heard.

Now is the time to give voice to the concerns of a younger population who have increasingly more to add to our present-day conversations as a society.

Sources

Generation Citizen. "Lowering the Voting Age for Local Elections in Takoma Park and Hyattsville, MD." October 2016. 22 March 2018.

Steinberg, Laurence. "A 16-Year-Old Is as Good as an 18-Year-Old—or a 40-Year-Old—at Voting." The Los Angeles Times. 3 November 2014. 26 March 2018.

Steinberg, Laurence. "Why We Should Lower the Voting Age to 16." The New York Times. 2 March 2018. 26 March 2018.

39 Am I Dangerous?

by Paige D. (2015)

I can consistently hit a 5" by 5" target at 350 yards with an AR-10 using a 6.5 Creedmoor round.

Am I dangerous?

My grandfather restored the M1 rifle that protected my great-grandfather in Normandy during World War II. We carry a history through this gun.

Are we dangerous?

I once heard a peer say that they would feel safer knowing the names and addresses of those with a legal firearms license—that they would know who to avoid. This comment—in response to a scandal where a county newspaper had actually done so—made me realize the true disconnect between those that understand firearms and those that don't. Consistently, responsible gun owners and criminals are grouped together in the firearm safety debate when this assumption is far from accurate.

One of the largest topics of debate is whether or not more legislation restricting the possession and ownership of firearms should be passed. It is believed by many that fewer firearms would reduce the number of children killed each year in our schools.

This is false.

A study done by the Harvard Journal of Law and Public Policy concludes that more guns equals less crime. It can also be noted that there is a strong correlation between cities with the highest armed crime rates and cities with the strictest gun laws. Yet the belief that less guns would be beneficial still stands. However, this is true to a certain degree—less illegal guns would be beneficial whereas less legal guns in the hands of responsible guns owners would be just the opposite.

Both those in favor of gun control and those that stand by the 2nd Amendment do agree on one stance, and a logical one at that. The mixture of mental illnesses and weapons should be heavily studied from a medical and psychological standpoint. Many instances of unprovoked and armed violence stem from a variety of psychological disorders. Currently, there is a misalignment in our system between identifying those with mental inhibitions and those restricted from purchasing, owning, or carrying firearms.

A New York Times article outlines a second flaw in the system where proper restrictions and scrutiny are not placed on proper individuals. The Bush Administration and other lawmakers pushed to have the terror watch list become valid criteria for being prohibited from legally purchasing firearms. However, this bill was not passed due to disorganization of said list and the possibility of alerting potential terrorists that they are being watched.

Why must misunderstanding make the most logical approaches and solutions void? Why must it be anecdotes and not logic that drive the debate and pondering over gun safety? Why must I be defined as dangerous?

Sources

Harvard Study–http://www.theacru.org/harvard_study_gun_control_is_counterproductive/

NY Times–http://www.nytimes.com/2015/02/26/opinion/gun-rights-for-terrorists.html

40 America First

by Safa Saleh, 17 (2017)

I am a refugee. Although I was not fully aware of what this meant at age 7, there are no words to describe the feelings that flooded over me when my family landed at Miami International Airport, when I realized that we were here to stay. The process of being accepted as a refugee into the United States is a nightmare. It took us 10 months of exhausting interviews, paperwork and medical tests. After fleeing Baghdad, and spending a year as illegal refugees in Jordan, that moment meant everything. It breaks my heart that in 2017, there are some trying to steal this moment from countless individuals whose promise of a new life will be broken—families no different from mine, who deserve a second chance but who won't get one. President Trump's executive order on immigration is not merely illegal and unconstitutional, but also heartless and discriminatory.

Under the newest draft of President Trump's executive order that is meant to "protect the nation from foreign terrorist entry," citizens from the affected countries—Iran, Somalia, Sudan, Yemen, Syria and Libya—will be subjected to a 90-day ban on travel to the United States. It should be noted that while Mr. Trump's ban covers these countries, which have produced exactly zero people linked to terrorist attacks that have killed Americans since 1975 to 2015, the ban does not cover countries like Turkey, Egypt, the United Arab Emirates and Saudi Arabia, with which the Trump family has business interests and whose citizens have been linked to terrorist attacks that have killed Americans. In addition to that, terrorism by Muslims as opposed to American Christian lone gunmen accounts for just one third of 1 percent of all murders in the United States.

But let's take a step back from the politics of it all. Children may die, families will be separated. These are the world's most vulnerable that we are turning our backs on. What about the tired, poor and huddled masses yearning to breathe free? A few weeks ago when returning to the United

States from Dubai, my family was selected for a "random security check." This one was more thorough than ever. I had to hold back tears as everyone in line passed while they were dissecting my bag like I was some sort of criminal. My crime? The American passport that I carry says that I was born in Iraq. My father asked the man why the security check was taking so much longer than usual. The man replied simply with "America first," but how do you put America first when you are destroying the very values it was founded upon?

Sources

Board, The Editorial. "Donald Trump's Muslim Ban Is Cowardly and Dangerous." The New York Times. The New York Times, 28 Jan. 2017. Web. 03 Apr. 2017.

"Executive Order: Protecting the Nation From Foreign Terrorist Entry Into the United States." The White House. The United States Government, 23 Feb. 2017. Web. 03 Apr. 2017.

Salama, Matthew Lee Vivian. "Donald Trump's 'Muslim Ban' to Be Re-Introduced with Iraq Removed from List of Countries." The Independent. Independent Digital News and Media, 01 Mar. 2017. Web. 03 Apr. 2017.

41 When You Are Old Enough to Vote, Will You?

by Ilana G. (2015)

A child I babysit once asked me out of the blue: "Aren't you excited to be 21?" He pretended to take a shot and descended into a fit of laughter. I immediately replied: "Nah, I'm excited to be 18. So I can vote." "Like that's exciting," he muttered.

My fourth grader's distaste for voting shocks me. When did voting become "un-cool"? The prospect of changing the government was enthralling, especially when I was young.

Turns out I was wrong. Earlier this year, I attempted to conduct a survey and a write subsequent article for my school's newspaper about political awareness. However, out of a student body of 700, only 54 people answered. When I inquired as to why they did not respond, many of the 646 other students often said "I'm not sure", "Who cares? I'm fine", and "Politics is just stupid". On my quest for statistics I received hesitancy, indifference, and snide.

If teenagers don't even want to spend four minutes on a survey, how can we expect them to participate in our electoral system? The numbers for the 18 to 29-year-olds shrink with each election; according to the census statistics, 45% voted in 2012 compared to 49% in 2008 (File and Crissey 5). Out of this select group, which hovers at 21% of our nation's population, approximately 11% of it votes in midterm elections (CIRCLE Staff 3). But the poor turnout in midterm elections makes for another article.

Charles M. Blow has every right to rage about this political detachment since "too many people shrug or sleep when they should seethe" (par 11). Whether it is Citizens United or disenfranchisement, too many issues target our civil liberties. The typical selfish Millennial Syndrome does not hinder the young vote; it's a crisis embedded in our electoral system. "Well, that's politics" can no longer be an excuse for our dissatisfaction. Ashley Spillane, President of Rock the Vote—an organization that engages the youth vote, says that despite youth's passion for prominent concerns, "Politics right now is really disheartening [. . . which is] why you see in the polls that young people are not affiliating with political parties" (Seipel par 10). Young people's enthusiasm for social action cannot replace the need for their intervention in government.

If you're dissatisfied, do something. If you're unsure, then wait. You don't have to vote now. Vote when you are the most informed democratic participant. Vote when you are confident of your decision's repercussions. Vote when you feel mature enough to say "I want to make a change". There's a fine line between indifference and insecurity; you can be on the latter's side.

I have my registration papers set for my 18th birthday. Do you?

Sources

Blow, Charles M. "We Should Be in a Rage." New York Times. New York Times, 9 April 2014. Web. 4 March 2015. http://nyti.ms/1kMtoTc

CIRCLE Staff. "The Youth Vote in 2010: Final Estimates Based on Census Data". Center for Information and Research on Civic Learning and Engagement. Civic Youth, 15 April 2011. Web. 6 March 2015. http://www.civicyouth.org/wp-content/uploads/2011/04/The-CPS-youth-vote-2010-FS-FINAL1.pdf

File, Thom and Sarah Crissey. "Voting and Registration in the Election of November of 2008". Current Population Reports, United States Census. Washington, July 2012. Web. 2015 5 March. http://www.census.gov/prod/2014pubs/p20-573.pdf

Seipel, Arnie. "Millennial Voters Are Paying Attention—So Why Don't More Vote?". NPR: It's All Politics. National Public Radio, 8 October 2014. Web. 5 March 2015. http://www.npr.org/blogs/itsallpolitics/2014/10/08/354187589/millennial-voters-are-paying-attention-so-why-don-t-more-actually-vot

42 I CAN'T HEAR YOU: Echo Chambers in America

by Kevin Tang, 16 (2018)

In 2018, America is more sharply divided than ever before as partisan animosity climbs to record highs during Trump's first year of presidency. Today, our political climate is marked by increasingly acerbic and polarizing rhetoric on all sides of the political spectrum. While we tend to blame those in Washington for splitting America into two, there is another major reason for this internal discord—ourselves. From social media to news outlets, we often shut ourselves in echo chambers that reinforce our existing views but exclude alternative views.

Understandably, we naturally do so in the first place because we like hearing what we want to hear and because we feel confident when others accept our opinions, especially when we browse through and post on social media. But, why is this specifically bad?

While some may contend that these platforms allow us to converse with like-minded individuals, echo chambers have silent, pernicious effects on the way we perceive truth. When we surround ourselves only with ideas that are similar to our own, we succumb to groupthink as we take everything we read as fact. This dangerous cycle perpetuates disinformation since we almost always don't take the time to independently verify what we read and view to be true in the echo chamber.

Statistical data already proves this phenomenon. In a 2016 study published in the Journal of Social and Political Psychology, Swedish researchers analyzed 700,000 posts on a right-wing forum. The results were shocking: It took only six months for the average user to adopt the community's radical opinions and go from "I" to "We."

Once we fall under the influences of this "mob mentality," we regard our beliefs as hard fact and refuse to engage in conflicting opinions, extinguishing civil discourse. For instance, when people of the same political affiliation were told to debate the merits behind denigrating rumors about the opposite party, the discussions notably veered toward reaffirming those erroneous statements.

Despite the plethora of multifaceted and diverse opinions offered online, we still overwhelming choose to latch onto narrow viewpoints that we want to hear. Instead of willfully ignoring the other side, we must learn to engage in opposing perspectives to listen and understand rather than to respond or scorn at. Instead of taking everything we read in blind faith, we must learn to analyze and question it.

So, at the end of the day, don't be afraid to question anything in life. Even if you feel like it's a "dumb" question, ask it. The more you learn, the less "dumb" questions you will have. But most importantly, learn to be prepared for the answer, too. It may not be what you want to hear, but that's the truth. The plain truth.

Sources

Bäck, Emma A., et al. "From I to We: Group Formation and Linguistic Adaption in an Online Xenophobic Forum." 13 March 2018. Journal of Social and Political Psychology. Accessed 24 March 2018.

DiFonzo, Nicholas. "The Echo-Chamber Effect." The New York Times, 22 Apr. 2011. The New York Times. Accessed 24 March 2018.

43 Discourse Is Democracy: Allowing Uncensored Speech on College Campuses

by Abigail Hogan, 17 (2017)

Christine Lagarde. Charles Murray. Condoleezza Rice. What do the director of the IMF, the conservative political scientist, and the 66th secretary of state have in common? All three have been prevented from speaking on college campuses due to student protests.

Campaigns by college students to block speakers from campus events have markedly increased in recent years. According to the Foundation for Individual Rights in Education, there have been 338 attempts by college students to prevent public figures from speaking at campus events since 2000. The annual number of "disinvitation events" has increased since 2011, with 2016 reaching a record high of 42 campaigns.

The protests themselves are not the problem. Throughout history, protests have been the catalyst for political progress, from Gandhi's salt march to the American Civil Rights movement. Instead, it is the motivation behind these college protests that provides a disservice to the students of today. Often, the reason for campaigns against speakers is the disparity between the politics or actions of the proposed speaker and the views of the student protesters. Many students hold that the beliefs of proposed speakers are so damaging that they should not be given a platform.

The solution to a difference of opinion is not a violent refusal to listen. Discourse is necessary.

By listening to and engaging with political opponents, students can strengthen their understanding of political issues and both sides can evolve their views.

In an increasingly polarized political climate, an understanding of opposing viewpoints is crucial to developing and strengthening one's own ideology. By listening to speakers with different political views, students are afforded the unique opportunity to learn about contrary beliefs and their underlying reasoning. In turn, this understanding allows students to refine their positions and, therefore, to more effectively advocate for them.

Vigorous and open debate also allows both sides the opportunity to engage in ideological development. One purpose of college is the ability to grow and change before venturing into the real world. Listening to a speaker with whom you already wholeheartedly agree is a merely a visit to the echo chamber. Exposure to new viewpoints may actually change the beliefs of students. Conversely, students who confront the speaker with informed questions and arguments may challenge the position of the speaker or sway other undecided listeners.

Thus, for the benefit of students and the future of political discourse, the practice of blocking speakers on college campuses must stop. College students should continue to protest, but should also listen and demand respectful dialogue with speakers, no matter their politics. If we fail to listen, if we turn our backs on the opposition instead of arguing and engaging, then we have already lost.

Sources

"Disinvitation Attempts." Foundation for Individual Rights in Education.

Fitzsimmons, Emma G. "Condoleezza Rice Backs Out of Rutgers Speech After Student Protests." The New York Times, 3 May 2014.

Pérez-Peña, Richard. "After Protests, I.M.F. Chief Withdraws as Smith College's Commencement Speaker." The New York Times, 12 May 2014.

Seelye, Katharine Q. "Protesters Disrupt Speech by 'Bell Curve' Author at Vermont College." The New York Times, 3 Mar. 2017.

44 Journalistic Objectivity Was Yesterday's Saving Grace

by Jeffrey W. (2015)

As an aspiring journalist, I thrive on facts. I am delighted by well-made infographics from nonpartisan research groups, quotes from primary sources and balanced articles from well-established media. As a Millennial, however, I was born and raised on the Internet.

With the democratization of information, anyone can become a journalist. For the first time in the history of written, daily news, the hierarchy of knowledge has been overturned. I, without leaving my desk, can report in detail the political views of villagers from Ayartharmam, India.

But this is not journalism. This is parlor talk. Though tense conversations exchanged over cups of cooling decaf have been replaced with social media diatribes, asserting their veracity with forked-tongued ferocity, the sources are still uncited, the details still misunderstood and the nuances still lost. Context and complexity have never had a place in these political arenas.

What has changed is the effect. In the past, these exchanges were ephemeral, dying at the doorway, forgotten on the drive home. Now, they linger, forever stored in the bizarre grandeur of the Internet.

Bloggers have become synonymous with reporters. These men and women, untrained and unqualified, have become the folk heroes of this new frontier. Their spin is heralded as innovative, rebellious and refreshing.

According to Ohio State Communications Professor, Silvia Knobloch-Westerwick, "People have more media choices these days, and they can choose to only be exposed to messages that agree with their current beliefs. . . . They're not looking for insights that might change their mind."

Glenn Greenwald, who broke the Snowden surveillance story, balks at objectivity. "Human beings are not objectivity-driven machines. We all intrinsically perceive and process the world through subjective prisms. What is the value in pretending otherwise?"

The value is freedom of thought. The truth of the matter is that information remains inaccessible. If we're lucky, we get second-hand news, harvested raw from an intrepid reporter for the Associated Press and refined by a major news outlet. More often, we get sensationalized, third-party headlines, regurgitated by colleagues, family and friends.

The facts back up Knobloch-Westerwick's finding. The Pew Research Center found the percentage of Americans expressing a consistently liberal or consistently conservative view has doubled, from 10% in 1994 to 21% in 2014.

Similarly, the portion of each party that believes that the other is a threat to the country has increased to 36 percent of Republicans and 27 percent of Democrats.

It is our job as journalists to deconstruct the hierarchy of knowledge, one article at a time. This won't be done by filtering the news through our opinion. It is our duty to pass down the information just as we found it, letting readers think for themselves.

Sources

Doherty, Carroll. "7 Things to Know About Polarization in America." Pew Research Center, 12 June 2014.

Grabmeier, Jeff. "Study: Americans Choose Media Messages That Agree with Their Views." The Ohio State University.

Keller, Bill. "Is Glenn Greenwald the Future of News?" New York Times, 27 Oct. 2013.

Sargunaraj, Wilbur. "How Did Obama Play In India? We Ask 4 Villagers To Weigh In." NPR, 27 Jan. 2015.

45 The Real Solution

by Kevin Morales, 17 (2016)

The fifteenth of March of the year 2016 was the day my father finally set foot on American soil for the first time in eleven years. It has been eleven years since America had told him he had to go, leaving behind his wife and three children. Last Tuesday, on a cloudy evening, my sister and I traveled to John F. Kennedy International Airport to pick up the man America has kept from us for so long. He never asked for this trouble; he just wanted one child to be born in New York so that one child would one day pull the family out of generations of poverty. What had to be done was done, and six months later I was born.

The current immigration system is broken, as it has been for many years, and denies many who want to become law-abiding the opportunity to do so. Deportation of the undocumented separates families and causes the loss of the prime workers of our economy, who are sent back to the places they wish to not be in anymore. Although many Americans have qualms about illegal immigration, there are about 12 million immigrants like my father who need immigration reform now.

The idea to make the perilous journey across the border just seems sensible in those who need to leave their country immediately. The Council on Foreign Relations reports that many of the undocumented come from countries ravaged by poverty and violence, such as Guatemala, Honduras and El Salvador. All of those coming into the country need to preserve their livelihood, but have to live under the accusation from Americans stating that "immigrants steal our jobs." In truth, as reported by The New York Times, immigrants enhance our economy. Therefore, America owes them for the taxes they pay with every purchase they make and the earned benefits they do not receive due to their status.

In addition, Congress needs to improve legal immigration, by accelerating visas for immigrants who are sponsored by family members. CNN reports the testimony of a woman who waited more than 13 years after being sponsored by the rest of her family, already living in the US, to finally be considered to come into the country.

Ironically, the resources that politicians suggest we can use to deport every illegal immigrant are the very resources that immigrants made possible for America to have. Families and children should not risk being deported and separated from each other. Congress should immediately pass immigration reform that reflects American family values. I lost my father for nearly my entire childhood and thankfully I have found him again. I hope other families will not have a similar experience.

Sources

Basu, Moni. "Waits for Immigration Status—the Legal Way—Can Be Long and Frustrating." CNN. Cable News Network, 9 Sept. 2014. Web. 23 Mar. 2016.

Davidson, Adam. "Debunking the Myth of the Job-Stealing Immigrant." The New York Times. The New York Times, 24 Mar. 2015. Web. 23 Mar. 2016.

Renwick, Danielle. "Central America's Violent Northern Triangle." Council on Foreign Relations. Council on Foreign Relations, 19 Jan. 2016. Web. 23 Mar. 2016.

Gender and Sexuality

"Periods have always been a cringeworthy topic."

"Start typing 'Alex Morgan' into YouTube and its first suggestion is 'Alex Morgan hot.'"

"Queer people are at a constant disadvantage, the door of opportunity isn't consistently open for us."

46 The Red Stain on Society

by Holly Keaton, 16 (2016)

The first time I got my period, I had no idea what to do. I woke up with stained sheets and a feeling of humiliation in my stomach; the night before, I had, embarrassingly enough, put a pad on the wrong way. I relied on the Internet to fix my mistakes, for I was far too ashamed to ask my mom for help or consult her in any way. I had suffered through Human Interaction like the rest of my peers, but it proved inadequate in the face of my anxiety and intense mortification. Periods have always been a cringeworthy topic—it would take me years before I could comfortably discuss them with my female friends, and years more for me to casually mention them to my male ones.

Menstruation has retained a slew of stigmas and misinformation; even though it is experienced by 50 percent of the world's population, the other half is often alarmingly uninformed about it. Tampons are seen as taboo objects; boys will stumble away from one as if menstruation is a disease they can catch. Not to mention that girls in India have been told that they will "pollute" food and "defile" idols while on their period, and some are even isolated into cowsheds for the duration of their cycle. This incredibly natural and normal and human cycle is too often universally treated like a disease, one that girls should feel shame and embarrassment about.

Perhaps the worst stigma associated with periods is that although they are considered unmentionable, men especially often use them to justify male superiority or to degrade and belittle women. Contrary to popular and misogynistic beliefs, the high levels of estrogen associated with menstruation actually deter women from impulsive decisions and increase synaptic connections with the hippocampus, the area of the brain related to short-term memory and decision-making, by 25 percent. So just because a woman's uterus is shedding its inner lining, it doesn't mean she is increasingly prone to rash and emotional decisions.

So because young girls across the world are petrified and embarrassed by a natural part of life; because the Internet taught me more about menstruation than school ever did; because boys are determined to avoid "period talk" even though they have sisters and mothers and girlfriends and friends who deal with it every month; because tampons and pads are taxed as luxury items, as though it's a luxury to have your period; because the number of euphemisms for "period" is overwhelming; because women's merits are disregarded in favor of "that time of the month" jokes, it's evident that periods need to not only be discussed, but also normalized and understood for what they are: simply another function of the human body.

Sources

Borreli, Lizette. "This Is Your Brain When You're on Your Period." Medical Daily. Medical Daily, 08 July 2015. Web. 19 Jan. 2016.

George, Rose. "The Taboo of Menstruation." The New York Times. The New York Times, 28 Dec. 2012. Web. 29 Mar. 2016.

47 Why I, a Heterosexual Teenage Boy, Want to See More Men in Speedos

by Noah Spencer, 17 (2014)

The Sports Illustrated Swimsuit edition recently celebrated its 50th birthday. As an 18-year old heterosexual male, I was happy to join in the festivities. However, one section of the magazine left me feeling something less than festive.

It wasn't the "Legends" section, featuring former models old enough to be my mother, nor the controversial photographs of Barbies in bathing suits (though that was pretty creepy). What upset me was the "Athletes" (pg. 196-205). Just two summers ago, I had watched Alex Morgan, star of the U.S. women's national soccer team, seize victory over the Canadian team in the Olympic semifinals with a gorgeous, heart-wrenching (for a Canadian) header in the 120th minute. Now I saw her posing seductively in a blue bikini, lumped together with dolls both plastic and flesh.

It wasn't Morgan (or W.N.B.A. star Skylar Diggins or surfer Anastasia Ashley) posing in the magazine that spawned my guilt. An athletically refined body is a source of great beauty and has cultural significance. In fact, my issue with the "Athletes" section wasn't with what it actually contained, it was with what it left out: Morgan et al.'s male counterparts.

Nowhere in this edition, nor in its 49 predecessors, was a male athlete photographed. By having exclusively female athletes model in scarce clothing, S.I. belittles their athletic accomplishments and serves to increase the gender inequality that is so widespread in sports.

Start typing "Alex Morgan" into YouTube and its first suggestion is "Alex Morgan hot"; click that and the top video on the page is one uploaded by "Sports Illustrated Swimsuit." (By contrast, the first suggestion that YouTube generates for "Cristiano Ronaldo," another world-class, attractive soccer player, is "Cristiano Ronaldo skills.") I can only imagine how dispiriting it must be for young girls who dream of becoming athletes to realize that even if they score a game-winning goal in the Olympics, their legacy will be more concerned with how they looked doing it.

According to The New York Times, the S.I. Swimsuit edition reaches millions of people worldwide. It has the power to influence readers' views of the athletes they feature. Currently, this power is being used to objectify women, but it doesn't have to be that way. My proposed solution is that Sports Illustrated rebrand their swimsuit issue to be similar to ESPN the Magazine's "Body Issue," focusing solely on athletes, male and female. By presenting the issue in this egalitarian method, athletes' bodies are celebrated for their beauty and S.I. is once again distributing magazines that are sports-related. Most importantly, the issue would no longer be contributing to the gender divide in sports, which would allow me to ogle Alex Morgan in good conscience.

Sources

Vega, Tanzina. "A New Swimsuit Issue Feature." The New York Times, 10 Feb. 2013.

North, Anna. "Put Ryan Lochte In the Sports Illustrated Swimsuit Issue." BuzzFeed, 12 Feb. 2013.

"Alex Morgan Body Painting—Swim Daily." YouTube, 2 July 2013. Sports Illustrated 2014 Swimsuit Edition.

48 Redefining Ladylike

by Zoie Taylore (2015)

"I did it five times."

"Well—I did it 12 times."

"I've got all of you beat. I did it 16 times!"

No—this isn't a scene from a raunchy high school movie, but rather a group of young women discussing how many times they've said the naughty word: sorry.

Saying sorry, especially for women, has become the new norm. As natural nurturers this instinctive space-filler keeps the peace, while simultaneously ensuring our likability and ladylikeness. This instant "belly up" tactic works to defeat women on a daily basis.

This "sorry" epidemic is detrimental to women, especially for the future of female leadership. According to the New York Times article "Speaking While Female", when a woman speaks in a professional setting, she walks a tightrope. This tightrope being the fine line between being barely heard, and being too aggressive. Speaking up puts you into the automatic bitch box. But not speaking up gets you nowhere, creating the ultimate female catch-22. This lexical faux pas could very well be the reason only 5.2 percent of Fortune 500 CEO's are women, and that women hold a mere 1 percent of the world's wealth.

Now, sorry in itself is not a bad word, nor is it gender exclusive. In fact, it is a common trait of politeness. And, according to a Salon article called "I'm Not Sorry for Saying Sorry: Women Should Feel Free to Apologize as Much as They Want," sorry is just a "ritual of restoring balance to a conversation." In other words, a form of chitchat to make people more comfortable. But constantly apologizing for speaking your mind, or for things that are not your fault is exhausting, incarcerating and usually exclusive to women.

Melissa Atkins Wardy, author of "Redefining Girly", recently stated in a CNN article that "Our girls need to learn their voice has every right to take up space in a conversation, in a room, and in an argument." Confidence counts just as much as competence and this generation of girls is lacking in one of the two. With 60 percent of all university graduates being women, it certainly isn't competence. And in addition, saying and feeling sorry for doing day-to-day activities causes a serious confidence gap between men and women. This is why men are more likely to feel over-confident, while women are prone to underestimation.

The recent Dove commercial "Sorry Not Sorry" has brought attention to the sorry sickness. With more women acknowledging the excessive use of this appeaser, the apology apocalypse will hopefully be a thing of the past.

"Women have been trained to speak softly and carry a lipstick. Those days are over."—Bella Abzug

Sources

ABC News. "Pantene Commercial Asks Whether Women Say 'Sorry' Too Much." ABC News, 18 June 2014. Web. 04 Mar. 2015.

Klingle, Kylah. "I'm Not Sorry for Saying Sorry: Women Should Feel Free to Apologize as Much as They Want." Salon, 12 July 2014. Web. 04 Mar. 2015.

Sandberg, Sheryl, and Adam Grant. "Speaking While Female." The New York Times, 10 Jan. 2015. Web. 04 Mar. 2015.

Wallace, Kelly. "Sorry to Ask but . . . Do Women Apologize More than Men?" CNN, 26 June 2014. Web. 04 Mar. 2015.

Warner, Judith. "Fact Sheet: The Women's Leadership Gap." Center for American Progress. 7 March 2014. Web. 11 Feb. 2015.

49 The Future of the #MeToo Movement Through the Eyes of a 17-Year-Old Boy

by Charles Gstalder, 17 (2018)

I'm Charlie, I'm 17, and I attend an all-male prep school. Discussions with my peers in the wake of the #MeToo movement have yielded shared feelings of disgust toward these abusers, and horror that we too may be part of the problem. This fear stems not from acknowledgment that we have facilitated harassment, but rather from the uncertainty of what constitutes reprehensible behavior.

Our shared worry was not spurred by Harvey Weinstein or Matt Lauer . . . , but instead from claims brought against Aziz Ansari. The allegations against Mr. Ansari appeared to be a landmark event, for instead of universally turning favor against him, they divided the community. Some notable feminists, including Bari Weiss, even began to back Ansari.

Following the release of the allegations Weiss published an article in The New York Times in which she calls for women to be more vocal about their wishes, and states that lumping Ansari in with other accused abusers "trivializes what the #MeToo movement first stood for." This sentiment was shared by my peers. Following the publication of the original exposé, my morning commute was dominated by debates over whether what Ansari did was wrong, and whether his accuser went too far. The fact that such discussions occurred is evidence of a systematic problem across the younger generations; we are unsure what exactly constitutes inappropriate sexual behavior.

The Economist recently published the results of a survey in which participants were asked whether they felt certain actions constituted sexual harassment. The findings were divided by nation, age and gender. The study concluded that in the U.S. there exists both a generational and gender gap. Older generations were shown to be less likely than younger generations to view actions such as commenting on attractiveness to be sexual harassment. Similarly, women were far more likely to view actions as harassment than their male counterparts. The divide demonstrated by the study coupled with the discourse surrounding Ansari paint a picture of a society confused, unsure and anxious. The only viable solution to such sentiments is further education.

I propose redefining sexual harassment and restructuring the way young men are taught about relationships. I believe that boys should be taught from a young age what is and is not acceptable, similarly to how young children are taught the difference between a "good touch" and a "bad touch." While I understand my claims may be viewed as shortsighted or worse, defensive of predators, my intent is the opposite. We young men know we are the problem and that until we change these issues will still occur. We want to be a part of the solution and long for education.

Sources

"Over-Friendly, or Sexual Harassment? It Depends Partly on Whom You Ask." The Economist, The Economist Newspaper, 17 Nov. 2017.

Weiss, Bari. "Aziz Ansari Is Guilty. Of Not Being a Mind Reader." The New York Times, The New York Times, 15 Jan. 2018.

50 How "It's Okay to Be Gay" Has Become a Lie in the Trump Era

by Lane Schnell, 16 (2019)

Straight people always seem to take delight in telling me, "It's 2019, no one cares if you're gay or trans!" As a lesbian, and a relatively socially-conscious one at that, I can confirm that this is a delusion of the highest order. Even if the individuals who claim this aren't overtly homophobic or transphobic, there are groups within the population who most definitely are. Namely: the current administration, who make it borderline dangerous to be a queer American.

Now, Trump supporters will immediately point to people like Peter Boykin, who runs "Gays for Trump," as evidence of mutual support between him and the LGBTQ community. However, this "evidence" is immediately counteracted by Trump's ban on transgender individuals serving in the military. Setting aside its nonsensical nature, the ban is yet another declaration of who the government feels are true citizens. Trump and the GOP have decided that trans people are too much of a "liability" to die for their country, and they're also trying to make it harder to even live in America and be LGBTQ.

A bill introduced to Congress on March 13, supposed to bring comprehensive anti-discrimination laws to the national level, will now likely fail, due to lack of Republican support. This mirrors the state-level situation, where only 20 states have specific legislation to prevent discrimination in employment, housing, and public accommodations/services. As Jodee Winterhoff of the Human Rights Campaign notes, "No one's civil rights should be dependent on what ZIP code they live in." Unfortunately, that's exactly the circumstance that many LGBTQ people are in currently, or will be at some point in their future.

Even smaller departments of the federal government are shifting in favor of anti-gay/trans policy. The current head of the Civil Rights Office at the Department of Health and Human Services is Roger Severino, a former civil rights attorney and outspoken critic of same-sex marriage. He has decried the LGBTQ community (falsely) for being "an ideology that's saying you can only go one way, against your biology," and he concurs with Trump's position on trans service members.

But perhaps the most dangerous and destructive policy that Severino has adopted aligns with his "conservative Christian" ideals: he believes that healthcare providers should be allowed to refuse care to gay or trans individuals if they have strong religious or moral objections to the patient's "lifestyle." This presents a special danger for the community, especially with violent hate crimes on the rise.

Queer people, therefore, are at a constant risk and disadvantage; the door of opportunity isn't consistently open for us. We all must continue to challenge the people in power who label LGBTQ lives worth less, because of who we are.

Sources

The Associated Press. "Push for Broader LGBT Rights Slowed by Lack of GOP Support." The New York Times, 12 Mar. 2019.

Green, Emma. "The Man Behind Trump's Religious-Freedom Agenda for Health Care." The Atlantic, 7 June 2017.

Pitofsky, Marina. " 'Epidemic of Violence': 2018 Is Worst for Deadly Assaults Against Transgender Americans." USA Today, 28 Sept. 2018.

"Roger Severino." GLAAD, 2018.

"United States: State Laws Threaten LGBT Equality." Human Rights Watch, 19 Feb. 2018.

51 You Don't Need to Glitter Things Pink to Get Me Into STEM

by Abby W. (2014)

As a high school junior interested in engineering, I am bombarded with emails and letters asking me to consider various STEM programs simply because I am female. Obviously, I am glad that so many colleges that are looking to increase the number of women enrolled in science and math related majors. However, I am somewhat alarmed by some of the tactics that some of these places use to attract potential female students. It appears that in order to make the STEM fields more attractive to girls, marketing directors feel the need to "feminize" these areas of study.

To me, this is just plain offensive. Is it assumed that I will only be interested in rebuilding the infrastructure of this nation via civil engineering if there is some sort of glittery pink aspect involved? Do people really think that the only way you will ever get a girl to write coding for innovative software is to stick a butterfly somewhere in there? These questions may seem far-fetched, but I have received far too many "lady-centric" emails in Curlz MT font from prospective colleges for that to be true.

And it isn't just colleges and universities that use these flawed tactics. Even toys targeted towards making little girls interested in engineering are feeling the need to "girlify" in order to make these activities appropriate for females. For instance, the famous LEGO company has started manufacturing kits for girls featuring beach houses and farmers' markets—things you certainly would not find in a regular, non-feminized LEGO kit. And I am not against toys meant to spark girls' interest in the STEM fields. What I am against is the seemingly ever-present stigmatization that the only way to create excitement in girls about traditionally male-dominated things is to bedazzle them with all things "female".

Women have always been interested in science and math, and this is proven by the presence of historical figures such as Marie Curie and Ada

Lovelace. So why are only a quarter of STEM jobs occupied by women? It's because for centuries, women were not welcomed into technical fields. However, painting rainbows onto fields of study such as engineering and computer science isn't going to magically make that statistic larger. What will attract more women to technical jobs is welcoming them with open arms and recognizing that their abilities are completely equal to that of men.

Of course, it is important to note that there is absolutely nothing wrong with a feminine engineer. But women aren't becoming scientists because the job application smelled like lavender. Many women are pursuing and will continue to pursue STEM careers because those are the topics that genuinely interest them.

Sources

Miller, Claire C. "A Day to Remember the First Computer Programmer Was a Woman." New York Times; Bits. New York Times, 15 Oct. 2013. Web. 09 Mar. 2014.

"Trends & Stats." Trends & Stats. Society of Women Engineers, n.d. Web. 09 Mar. 2014.

52 The Question Up For Debate: Is Feminism Really For Everyone?

by Nico Mayer, 14 (2016)

The public needs a broader representation of feminism than what mainstream media has provided. Women like Patricia Arquette and Emma Watson have been spotlighted for speaking out on women's issues, however, rarely do women who don't share their white, upper-class experience receive the attention that is needed to manifest the true goal of feminism.

Intersectionality acknowledges that feminism is not one-size-fits-all, that each aspect of a woman's identity (what "sections" she fits into) contribute to her experience. For example, race, ethnicity, religion, economic status, ability, and sexual orientation are all contributors to the privilege a person might or might not have. According to the ideas of Kimberlé Crenshaw, a black woman who introduced the intersectional theory, " . . . the intersectional experience is greater than the sum of racism and sexism, any analysis that does not take intersectionality into account cannot sufficiently address the particular manner in which Black women are subordinated."

One example of typical "one-size-fits-all" feminism or "white feminism" is the way the wage gap is discussed. The most common number heard in this discussion is that women make 78 cents to every white man's dollar. However, this number is only true for white women. In reality, the wage gap for women and all people of color is even greater. For African-American women that number lowers to 64 cents, and for Latina women 54 cents.

According to Jarune Uwujaren and Jamie Utt for the website Everyday Feminism, "between 25 percent and 50 percent of women experience gender-based violence (sexual violence, intimate partner violence, street harassment or stalking) in their lifetime." However, as further explained by Uwujaren and Utt, using an intersectional lens reveals the whole story.

Similar to using 78 cents to represent the wage gap, limiting statistics about gender-based violence without considering other factors besides gender disguises important trends in the data to which we as a society need to pay attention. For instance, although all women are at risk, bisexual women are far more likely to experience sexual violence. Understanding the difference in frequency and risk will help us better protect and find more justice for women.

Some may object to an intersectional approach because it preserves differences. Some feel that intersectionality divides women—comments like "why do you have to bring up race?" and "doesn't this pit women against each other?" are examples of this position. However, acknowledging real differences doesn't create them. Instead, the recent popularization of intersectional feminism has offered a way for all women to be there for each other and to find strength through their own differences.

Sources

Caraminca, Jon. "Nicki Minaj and Meek Mill, Twitter's Ethics Police." The New York Times 24 July 2015: n. pag. Web.

Crenshaw, Kimberlé. "Demarginalizing the Intersection of Race and Sex: A Black Feminist Critique of Antidiscrimination Doctrine, Feminist Theory, and Antiracist Politics." (n.d.): n. pag. Web.

"NISVS Infographic." Centers for Disease Control and Prevention. Centers for Disease Control and Prevention, 08 Sept. 2014. Web. 22 Feb. 2016.

"NISVS Infographic." Centers for Disease Control and Prevention. Centers for Disease Control and Prevention, 08 Sept. 2014. Web. 22 Feb. 2016.

"Unfair Pay for Women and People of Color." Eideard. N.p., 23 Oct. 2014. Web. 22 Feb. 2016.

Uwujaren, Jarune, and Jamie Utt. "Why Our Feminism Must Be Intersectional (And 3 Ways to Practice It)." Everyday Feminism. N.p., 11 Jan. 2015. Web. 22 Feb. 2016.

53 Under Black Cloaks

by Bincheng Mao, 16 (2018)

Can you imagine a life in which you are merely the property of someone else? Unfortunately, this is exactly the life of women in Saudi Arabia, where the treatment of women restricts their fundamental human rights.

During my two years living in Dubai and Qatar, I went to Saudi Arabia three times with my father where I witnessed their discriminatory policies. In a mall in Riyadh, I was shocked to see a woman awkwardly eating noodles without taking off the veil of her niqab. She used a fork to lift the noodles toward the eye-opening, and slightly pulled the lower part away from her face, then pointed the fork down so the noodles would slide onto the inside of the veil without revealing her face.

As it turns out, the Saudi government strictly prohibits women in public from ever taking off their niqabs. Saudi Arabia claims these restrictions are to ensure "women's modesty" commanded by Allah. Yet, not only are these restrictions undignifying, the Quran calls for "both men and women 'to cover and be modest.'" The fact that the Saudi government only restrict women reveals a double standard.

However demeaning the requirement of wearing a niqab in public might be, it is only one symptom of a system that restricts women's fundamental rights. According to Human Rights Watch, Saudi females' lives are controlled by male guardians from birth to death due to its unique guardianship system. As hundreds of Saudi females have attested, this is a most inhumane policy as the male guardian decides whether "his" woman can see a doctor or even leave prison. Presumably, Saudi leadership, composed entirely of men, believes that women are unable to make the types of decisions that men make. Over time, the system gradually changes Saudi women's mind-sets, reducing them to men's property, even in their hearts. Rania, a 34-year-old Saudi woman, said, "We are entrusted with raising the next generation but you can't trust us with ourselves. It doesn't make any sense."

While the Saudi government argues that these policies are protecting women, they have nothing to do with protection and everything to do with dehumanization. However, President Trump has proposed multiple economic collaborations with Saudi Arabia, and during his recent meeting with Prince Salman, "over 20 people were at the table, yet none were women." This symbolic irony along with other policies reveal the U.S. government's unwillingness to address this gender disparity.

It is time for our free nation to push for urgently-needed reforms by placing conditions of ending human rights violations to U.S.-Saudi trade deals. Instead of ignoring these human rights abuses, the United States of America should show the world that abuses are not tolerated.

Sources

"Boxed In: Women and Saudi Arabia's Male Guardianship System." Human Rights Watch, 6 June 2017.

Cochrane, Emily. "Over 20 People Were at the Table When Trump Met the Saudis. None Were Women." The New York Times, 21 Mar. 2018.

Mythili Sampathkumar. "Nine Members of the UN Human Rights Council Accused of Violating Human Rights." The Independent, 21 Sept. 2017.

"The United Nations Human Rights Office of the High Commissioner Annual Report." OHCHR, 7 Mar. 2017.

Vyver, James. "Explained: Why Muslim Women Wear a Burka, Niqab or Hijab." ABC News, 17 Aug. 2017.

54 Why We Must Act on #MeToo

by Bhargavi Garimella, 17 (2018)

In 1997, Tarana Burke was working at a youth camp when a 13-year-old girl told Ms. Burke that her stepfather had been sexually abusing her. Tarana was left speechless—what could she tell the girl, and hundreds of others in her position, that would convey that she understood and felt their pain? Ten years after that conversation, Ms. Burke finally found what she needed to say: me too.

As a survivor of child sexual assault, I have been waiting for these two words for a very long time—seeing the #MeToo movement explode empowered me to share my experiences with others after years of being silent. The #MeToo movement brought me to a place in which I felt that I could openly discuss my experience without judgment or victim blaming. Saying #MeToo is a statement of understanding like no other. But what must remain fundamental is that the movement is about more than awareness and empathy. It is also about changes to laws and policies that perpetuate the imbalance of power between men and women. It is about challenging social norms and a culture in which the victim is instinctively blamed for the crime.

This issue requires us, as a society, to examine ourselves and our culture that allows and encourages this type of behavior. At some point, we must ask ourselves if the "problem" of sexual assault is an unintended consequence or the purposeful product of a system designed to systematically isolate, silence and marginalize those with lesser power. A report from the U.S. Equal Employment Opportunity Commission found that 75 percent of workplace harassment incidents go unreported—for those who did speak out, 75 percent faced retaliation from their employer. A matter of such magnitude cannot be mended on a case-by-case basis.

Comprehensively fixing this issue starts with providing women effective reporting options beyond filing a complaint with HR or talking to their managers—options that often have only the company's best interest at heart—and giving women decision-making roles in which they have the same chance for success as men.

Although the #MeToo movement is not exempt from criticism, those who call it a "moral panic" are misdiagnosing it. What #MeToo is is a social movement that finally holds powerful men accountable for their actions; as author David Perry writes, #MeToo is not an act of persecution, but rather a rebellion against the powers that persecute. In order for our culture to change and in order for future generations to grow up in an equitable world, we must build on #MeToo as a vehicle for reform in our courts, workplaces and schools. It is a wake-up call and an opportunity to inspire genuine change—an opportunity that we cannot waste.

Sources

Beck, Richard. "#MeToo Is Not a Witch Hunt." Vox. 11 Jan. 2018.

Bennett, Jessica. "The #MeToo Moment: No Longer Complicit." The New York Times. 7 Dec. 2017.

Campbell, Alexia Fernandez. "How the Legal System Fails Victims of Sexual Harassment." Vox. 30 March 2018.

Garcia, Sandra. "The Woman Who Created #MeToo Long Before the Hashtag." The New York Times. 20 Oct. 2017.

Golshan, Tara. "Study Finds 75 Percent of Workplace Harassment Victims Experienced Retaliation When They Spoke Up." Vox. 15 Oct. 2017.

Gorman, Michele. "1 in 4 Women Experienced Sexual Assault in College, Survey Finds." Newsweek. 21 Sept. 2015.

Guerra, Cristela. "Where'd the 'Me Too' Initiative Really Come From? Activist Tarana Burke, Long Before Hashtags." The Boston Globe. 17 Oct. 2017.

Klein, Ezra. "When a Culture Produces This Much Sexual Assault, It's Not an Accident." Vox. 23 Oct. 2017.

North, Anna. "Want to Stop Sexual Harassment? Start Helping Women." Vox. 9 Nov. 2017.

Perry, David. "No, #MeToo Is Not a Witch Hunt." Pacific Standard Magazine. 9 Jan. 2018.

55 Egghead Son vs. Airhead Daughter?

by Rachel S. and Nancy B. (2015)

"Honey, I hope our son blossoms into a handsome man so he's sure to find a successful wife who supports his family while he is Mr. Mom. And I hope our daughter is gifted enough to land herself a high-paying executive job to support her loyal husband and the kids." Yeah right.

Despite the progress made in women's rights, parents still have varying hopes for their sons versus their daughters, with only our cultural stereotypes to blame.

These different expectations may not show in person, but parents have no problem sharing them with the internet. In "Google, Tell Me. Is My Son a Genius?" Davidowitz reveals that "for every 10 U.S. Google queries about boys being overweight, there are 17 about girls," even though boys prove "9 percent more likely to be overweight." In addition, "for every 10 queries about girls being gifted, there are 25 about boys" despite the fact that girls are "11 percent more likely to be in a gifted program." The concept that parents truly hope for, the classic thin, beautiful woman and the strong intelligent man, seems to be the juxtaposition nowadays.

People may claim that expectations between sons and daughters are equal because of girls' major advancements throughout the years: Sarah Palin running for vice president, Barbara Walters co-anchoring a news show, Danica Patrick racing in NASCAR. Girls are overcoming barriers and making names for themselves. Opportunities are more equal than ever before. Yes, that may be true, but data reveals parents still desire to have a smart boy and pretty girl. As Erin Ryan mentioned, "No matter who we are, and where we live, it's impossible to escape the pervasive message that women are more valuable when they're more decorative and men are more valuable when they're the ones doing the thinking and deciding." Our culture illustrates this everywhere from books we read to movies we watch, like Cinderella which shows how beauty helps evade indigence and be swept away by a wealthy, intelligent man. Obviously, many girls still wish to graduate with an "MRS degree", and many guys still wish to prosper enough to support a family. But those are the children's wishes, not the parents worrying about dictating labels.

Those believing gender inequality simply isn't concerning anymore ought to compare men's and women's salaries. The Pew Research Center verifies "women earn 84 percent of what men earn." Simple facts display that despite all the progress made, our culture encourages men to have the brains over women.

Should society still worry about our sons being egghead brainiacs and our daughters being airhead beauty queens? Or is it time to finally defy society's cultural stereotypes by encouraging intelligence and beauty for both genders?

Sources

Ryan, Erin G. "Parents Hope Their Sons Are Geniuses and Their Daughters Aren't Fat." Jezebel. N.p., 22 Jan. 2014. Web. 06 Mar. 2015. http://jezebel.com/parents-hope-their-sons-are-geniuses-and-their-daughter-1506826763?utm_campaign=socialflow_jezebel_facebook&utm_source=jezebel_facebook&utm_medium=socialflow.

Stephens-Davidowitz, Seth. "Google, Tell Me. Is My Son a Genius." New York Times. New York Times, 18 Jan. 2014. Web. 05 Mar. 2015. http://www.newyorktimes.com/2014/01/19/opinion/sunday/google-tell-me-is-my-son-a-genius.html.

Patten, Eileen. "On Equal Pay Day, Key Facts about the Gender Pay Gap." Pew Research Center RSS. Pew Research Center, 08 Apr. 2014. Web. 06 Mar. 2015. http://www.pewresearch.org/fact-tank/2014/04/08/on-equal-pay-day-everything-you-need-to-know-about-the-gender-pay-gap/.

Race and Religion

"Growing up, the hijab always puzzled me."

"Humans don't need religion to be moral."

"Painting all Asians with the brush of the model minority—assimilatory and successful—is not only false, but dangerous."

56 The Asian Misnomer: What the Affirmative Action Debate Misses

by Matteo Wong, 16 (2017)

One Scantron bubble and five letters: "Asian." That's all the College Board needs to encompass the heritage of thousands of students and 48 countries. Those five letters are also what many college admissions officers use as the basis for establishing diversity through affirmative action. While some institutions provide options such as "Chinese," "Asian Indian" and "Other Asian," a glance at official demographics reports shows that they don't actually care; all of these ethnicities are still homogenized as Asian.

Proponents of affirmative action commonly argue that diversity improves critical thinking, creativity and race relations. Colleges like Caltech, which enrolled 42 percent Asians in 2016, are then doing a disservice to their students by not exposing them to a variety of perspectives. This train of thought assumes that all "Asians" have similar cultural values, namely prioritizing academic achievement and exam scores.

Painting all Asians with the brush of the model minority—assimilatory and successful—is not only false, but dangerous. Though 72 percent of Indian-Americans and 53 percent of Chinese-Americans have a college degree, Hmong-, Laotian-, and Cambodian-Americans drop out of high school at rates approaching 40 percent. Grouping Muslim- and Chinese-Americans makes them both appear well-adjusted on paper, but in person Muslims are faced with severe xenophobia. Even if Chinese- and Indian-Americans have an unfair advantage in college admissions, lumping all Asians with them causes underprivileged Asian subgroups to not receive the attention and government services they need.

More shockingly, Bangladesh, Myanmar and China are not the same place; progressive Americans seem to think Democrats and Republicans have different countries of origin, yet they assume Muslim-, Burmese-, and Chinese-Americans all live in Confucian homes and celebrate Chinese New Year.

In fact, the Muslims in Bangladesh celebrate Eid, in Myanmar people throw water during Thingyan, and neither country places a heavy emphasis on Confucian values; do not conflate Asian with Chinese. Asia encompasses a series of rich, complex cultures, and claiming a high concentration of Asians will destroy on-campus diversity is not only false, but erases the unique perspectives offered by Asian students.

Promoting racial diversity is undoubtedly important to college campuses, but the definition of diversity is flawed. Asians are not a monolith, and should not be treated as such; schools should actively recognize all 48 linguistic groups currently encompassed by "Asian." This is not to single out Chinese students as the problem, but rather to remedy affirmative action's unfair discrimination against disadvantaged Asian subgroups. Understanding the intricacies of "Asian America" would allow college admissions officers to create richer on-campus diversity, while simultaneously granting visibility, and potentially economic or social aid, to underrepresented "Asians."

Sources

Chang H, Sharon. "The Growing Poverty Crisis That Everyone Is Ignoring." ThinkProgress. 27 Sep. 2015.

Saulny, Susan and Steinberg, Jacques. "On College Forms, a Question of Race, or Races, Can Perplex." The New York Times. 13 June 2011.

Bollinger, Lee C. "Affirmative Action Isn't Just a Legal Issue. It's Also a Historical One." The New York Times. 24 June 2016.

Progress 2050. "Who Are Asian Americans?" 28 April 2015.

Office of the Registrar. "Fall Enrollment 2016-17." Caltech. N.d.

Ramakrishnan, Karthick. "National Origin Data Would be Helpful in Understanding Asian-Americans." 16 Oct. 2015.

57 Muddying a Sacred Cloth: When the Hijab Is Worn in Solidarity

by Zahra Nasser, 17 (2016)

Growing up, the hijab always puzzled me. At the mosque, the other little girls my age tugged at their mothers' hijabs and burqas, and did so on the way home, too. My mom's hijab and burqa was fleeting; it was on in the mosque, but gone as soon as she stepped foot out of the domed building. That confused me. It's taken time for me to realize that every Muslim woman faces making this choice and the consequences that result from it.

When Larycia Hawkins, a Christian political science professor at Wheaton College, wore the hijab to show "solidarity" with Muslim women, she fell victim to different kinds of consequences: theological arguments, general anger from non-Muslims and protest from Muslim women about the true meaning of being a hijabi. Hawkins's eventual suspension from Wheaton College resulted from her views about Muslims and Christians believing in one same God, which went against the college's views. But neither Wheaton College nor the Council on American-Islamic Relations objected to her physical display.

To Muslim women, though, the physical gesture itself was provocative. The New York Times organized a Room for Debate on the question, "Do Non-Muslims Help or Hurt Women by Wearing Hijabs?," inviting Muslim women from various backgrounds to share their thoughts. The range of responses was vast. Some debaters argued that the hijab symbolizes oppression, citing scarring childhood experiences growing up in Muslim countries. Others applauded Hawkins, welcoming the expression of solidarity, but suggesting solidarity should not stop there.

Reading through each contributor's views, it occurred to me the disservice Hawkins actually committed: She perpetuated the infamous divide between hijabi and non-hijabi by picking a side in a fight that isn't hers. Hawkins may wear the hijab to express support, but she has the luxury of taking the hijab off when she pleases. In many cultures, Muslim women are disowned, threatened by the prospect of never finding a husband, or physically abused when their hijab comes off.

Hawkins's intention to combat Islamophobia is admirable, but wearing the hijab isn't the only way to do so. If society wants to express true solidarity with Muslim women, it must stand with all Muslim women—hijabi and non-hijabi, those who wear mini skirts as well as the fully veiled, the stay-at-home mom as well as the academic.

I remember asking my mom why she didn't wear a hijab like most of my Muslim peers' moms did. She responded: "A cloth draped on my head doesn't make me a Muslim. We are all Muslim in different ways." It'll take time for Muslims and non-Muslims alike to embrace this diversity, but when we do, we will truly be in solidarity.

Sources

Graham, Ruth. "The Professor Suspended for Saying Muslims and Christians Worship One God." The Atlantic. 17 Dec. 2015.

Hindustan Times correspondent. "Father kills 4-year-old daughter for not covering her head." The Hindustan Times. 3 Oct. 2015.

Nomani, Asra and Arafa, Hala. "As Muslim Women, We Actually Ask You Not to Wear the Hijab in the Name of Interfaith Solidarity." The Washington Post. 21 Dec. 2015.

"Room for Debate: Do Non-Muslims Help or Hurt Women By Wearing Hijabs?" The New York Times. 6 Jan. 2016.

58 Indigenous: Unheard, But Loud

by Marco Alvarez, 16 (2016)

When I was young, I was raised with television and movies giving me an image of Native Americans, showing me that they always wore feathers, wore only loin cloths, couldn't comprehend English, and were barbaric savages. I am a Lipan Apache. I guess I don't fit the "Indian" mold.

Growing up, I have always watched sports, especially football. When I was very young, I remember watching a Washington Redskins game for the first time. That day will forever be engraved in my mind. I saw people with red paint smothered over their whole face, wielding tomahawks, and wearing fake headdresses. This is the modern "black face," the modern blind racism. And there needs to be an end to this.

A problem that has silently plagued America for quite some time is the mistreatment of Native Americans. Native Americans are constantly mocked by media and shunned by the government. Written in the American Declaration of Independence, indigenous people are referred as "merciless Indian Savages." Teen suicide and infant mortality are rampant problems throughout the reservations. According to The New York Times, native youth have the highest suicide rate of any United States ethnic group and natives suffer from infant mortality 60 percent higher than Caucasians. According to the Center on Juvenile and Criminal Justice, indigenous people are more likely than any other racial groups in the United States to be killed by police. One case is the killing of John T. Williams of the Nuu-chah-nulth tribe. John was a mentally ill 50 year old man, deaf in one ear, who carved wood for a living. John was shot four times by a police officer within seconds of dropping a knife and a piece of cedar he was carving. He died; the folding knife was found closed on the ground.

We have the power to unravel these dilemmas and to truly fix them. The main root of these problems is the lack of knowledge and recognition. The casual American most likely wouldn't know that the name "Redskin" is a term for native bounty gained. The casual American most likely wouldn't know that native people are calling for help from the ruins of the reservations. The casual American most likely wouldn't know that natives are second and third class citizens in their own lands. We have the power to solve this, but we haven't taken big enough steps yet. Nothing has ever started without someone acting upon it. If we could resolve these predicaments, we could make peace with the tribes and government. Natives are constantly calling for help, but are continuously overlooked. Indigenous people protest their spirits out onto the road, but they are quickly consumed by the hum of American traffic.

Sources

Records Administration, n.d. Web. 08 Dec. 2015.

"Language Log.": The Origin of Redskin. N.p., n.d. Web. 08 Dec. 2015.

"Native Lives Matter, Too." The New York Times. N.p., n.d. Web. 08 Dec. 2015.

"Who Are Police Killing?" Center on Juvenile and Criminal Justice. N.p., n.d. Web. 08 Dec. 2015.

59 Good Before God (or Any of His Religions)

by Jason Barr, 16 (2016)

Ever since my introduction to the world of Scouting, I have been 99 percent on board. Through the program I have met people, gotten opportunities, and learned lessons that I would have otherwise never been exposed to. Their ideals and moral code are mostly wonderful. Just one little thing bothers me: "Do my duty to God and my country." God was never a part of my life before I learned this line. Why does he have to be now? Why does Scouting, and society in general, tag "reverent" on to the end of their moral code? This is counterintuitive: Humans don't need religion to be moral.

In fact, recent research suggests that on a psychological level "niceness" goes beyond religion and even humanity. According to The New York Times article "Good Without God?", other mammals such as chimpanzees have been seen to act in kind ways benefiting society. The article describes instances such as younger monkeys bringing water to an older arthritic monkey, and primates refusing to take rewards greater than are offered to their cohorts. Chimps aren't the only ones: Dogs and mammals in general have been shown to act in ways that benefit their communities as a whole. Prospect Magazine has quoted British psychologist Margaret Knight explaining how humans, like all mammals, "are naturally social beings." Thus, life is more positive and fulfilling for all if members of a community act in a friendly and cooperative manner.

I can hear you now: "So what if animals are 'nice,' that doesn't make them moral." Okay, true. "Nice" is not synonymous with "moral." However, morality is derived almost directly from simple ideas of goodness. The Scout Law, a sort of definition of the ideal Scout's personality, is based off of simple, one word traits: "friendly," "helpful," "courteous." These traits aren't divine commands from deities or inspired writings of prophets: They're traits any old Joe would use to describe a neighbor or friend. Morals do not stem from the divine, they come from more basic things, such as a need for a society to be happy. If morals are indeed a basic lubricant of society, then existing without religion isn't existing without morals.

Sources

Antony, Louise M. "Good Minus God." Opinionator Good Minus God Comments. The New York Times, 18 Dec. 2011. Web. 09 Mar. 2016.

Coopson, Andrew. "To Lead a Moral Life We're Better off without Religion | Prospect Magazine." Prospect Magazine, 12 Feb. 2016. Web. 10 Mar. 2016.

De Waal, Frans. "Morals Without God?" Opinionator Morals Without God Comments. The New York Times, 17 Oct. 2010. Web. 10 Mar. 2016.

Leonhardt, David. "The Rise of Young Americans Who Don't Believe in God." The New York Times. The New York Times, 12 May 2015. Web. 11 Mar. 2016.

60 Intelligence Over Diversity

by Ashley K. (2014)

Many college campuses in the United States are working diligently to create diverse learning environments for people of all racial and ethnic backgrounds. In June 2013, the Supreme Court issued a ruling that the use of diversity in the admission process for public universities not only provides educational and social benefits but also promotes the ideal of America being one, indivisible nation. The use of diversity in applications, known as affirmative action, does provide the benefits of social diversity. However, despite its purpose to remove the threat of racial prejudices, affirmative action is simply creating a new bias and should not be implemented in college applications.

Instead of withholding benefits from minorities, the tables have been turned to ensure that minorities hold an advantage over the majority of white Americans. At what point can racial discrimination end? When can all people be simply viewed as equal individuals where race and ethnicity are no longer acknowledged?

On college campuses, I agree that diversity is an important aspect of growing more socially and culturally aware. However, I believe that basing the acceptance of applicants on their race rather than their academic achievements weakens the idea of gaining a higher education and is truly unfair to applicants of all racial and ethnic groups. The point of attending a university is to gain wisdom and knowledge, not to spend time with the most diverse group of people that can be gathered together.

I, as a Pacific Islander, have always benefited from the implementation of affirmative action, and yet I am appalled by the idea of being given an advantage in college admissions based strictly on the ethnicity with which I identify. I am constantly frustrated that I may only have been accepted to certain institutions based on nothing more than the fact that I will help fulfill their diversity proportion. I may never know if my academics alone, without my ethnicity, would have been sufficient for me to attend a prestigious university. Instead, I feel as if all of my achievements are demeaned because of my identification with a non-white ethnicity and judged by others who may believe that I was only accepted to certain universities because of my ethnicity and not my academic standings.

Yes, diversity is important. No, maintaining a diverse college campus is not more imperative than providing an academically rich campus. Yes, racial prejudice should be avoided. No, the current system of affirmative action is not preventing bias based on ethnicity. Affirmative action is simply a new, socially acceptable form of racial prejudice. Colleges need to stop focusing on diversity in order to judge applicants fairly in their qualities and character rather than their color.

Sources

The Editorial Board. "A Reprieve for Affirmative Action." The New York Times, 24 June 2013.

Toppo, Greg. "Affirmative Action Fading From College Scene." USA Today, 12 Feb. 2014.

"Affirmative Action." The Leadership Conference on Civil and Human Rights.

61 The Missing Anthropological Exhibit at the Museum of Natural History

by Alec Farber, 16 (2017)

The American Museum of Natural History serves 5 million visitors annually, ranging from elementary schools to foreign tourists. Although massive displays like the dinosaur halls are famous draws, the museum is also well known for its anthropological exhibits, which include the Hall of Asian Peoples, the Hall of African Peoples, and so forth. However, for 148 years, the museum has decided to not create a hall for Europeans. The museum, in order to present visitors an updated view of anthropology, must add a Hall of European Peoples.

The idea of more European culture in our institutions can sound unnecessary, and even racist, to many. But before judging, ask yourself: What are the consequences of portraying Europeans as above anthropology? When only people of color are exhibited in the museum, visitors learn that there must be something intrinsically different about European culture. The exhibits teach this because they are rooted in a white, 19th century worldview. Although updated, the exhibits still reflect a time when European artifacts were considered "art" or "history," while other artifacts were labeled "natural history." The museum's European superiority was so extreme that, in 1897, six Eskimos were displayed solely as "a source of amusement" for visitors. Such racism in anthropology was common at a time when anything European was considered "civilization," while anything else was labeled "primitive."

Admirably, anthropologists have worked for years to replace racism with more modern principles. These principles include that all cultures are equal and deserve respect, and that anthropologists shouldn't label a culture "primitive" just because they are different. What the museum has not done, by excluding Europe from display, is teach visitors that all cultures deserve the same level of scientific scrutiny. The truth is that anthropology should apply to all cultures, and no ethnicity should be above scientific study. Margaret Mead once said that "the more complex a society becomes, the more fully the law must take into account the diversity of the people who live in it." I would argue that the more complex our view of culture becomes, the more fully our institutions must take into account the diversity of the people who visit.

If the museum is truly for all people, then it must be about all people. There is nothing intrinsically different between Europe's culture and that of the rest of the world. All cultures are equally complex and impressive. The only reason to isolate the study of Europe from the rest of the world would be because Europe is somehow special, something we know to be false. European culture is unique, but not uniquely superior.

Yet, until Europeans are included in the Museum's Anthropological Halls, visitors will learn otherwise.

Sources

Kaufman, Michael T. "About New York: A Museum's Eskimo Skeletons and Its Own." The New York Times. August 21, 1993.

Popova, Maria. "Margaret Mead on the Root of Racism and the Liability of Law Enforcement." brainpickings.org. 2014.

Science, Technology, and the Environment

"I recently underwent a teenage rite of passage: beginning to drive."

"There are too many cases of state legislatures, school districts and teachers actively denying the fact that climate change is real."

"By informing you of this ongoing crisis, am I telling you to give up seafood? Never!"

62 Nothing Gets Between Me and My Sushi . . . Except Plastic, Maybe

by Sophia Lee, 15 (2019)

As an Asian-American self-proclaimed millennial foodie, imagine the shock I experienced when I discovered a horrifying truth—plastic cuisine. Ubiquitous plastic extends beyond our surroundings—and invades our guts—through what we eat and drink. I first learned that sushi is chock-full of microplastics. There's so much plastic in the water, churned down to the size of rice grains or smaller, and fish gobble it up. When the fish end up on our dinner plates, guess what? Our bellies receive an unsettling supplement that wasn't on the menu.

In fact, a National Geographic study found microplastics in 114 marine species—with over half of them regulars in restaurants—meaning that my tummy acquires some uninvited non-digestible additives.

Even water isn't safe! My parents often tell me to drink more water to wash down my food—but did they know that I was ingesting plastic too? A 2017 study by Orb Media found microplastic contamination in 83 percent of global tap water—with the highest amount, 94 percent, found in the United States!

You may wonder: So what? Has there been a study that proves housing microplastics inside of your body is harmful? Not yet, but still. Firstly—it's gross! I'm eating a material that's meant to last beyond a thousand years, and will probably accompany my skeleton long after I putrefy in my grave.

Imagine the surplus of chemicals needed to make these durable particles. National Geographic highlighted a few chemicals contained in plastic with the potential to become poisons in certain doses: "endocrine disruptors—chemicals that interfere with normal hormone function, even contribute to weight gain. Flame retardants may interfere with brain development in fetuses and children; other compounds that cling to plastics can cause cancer or birth defects."

By informing you of this ongoing crisis, am I telling you to give up seafood? Never!

Personally, and I think I can speak for many fellow foodies, nothing gets in between me and my sushi. Instead, let's stop dismissing the old-school motto: reuse, reduce, and recycle. Seriously—no more Acme bags that drift yonder with the wind, and take a hint from good ol' Trader Joes for the more environmentally friendly alternatives. Sure, paper bags may be more fragile, and fabric ones are often more expensive, but that's a small price to pay for potentially saving a sea creature that would have been strangled or starved otherwise.

Let's cut down on the plastic, and the next time you're tempted to innocuously trash some plastic straws, just remember that same "harmless" plastic is somewhere puncturing a turtle's brain through its nostril and killing a fish through literally explosive bowels . . . and its next stop?

Your stomach.

Sources

Kosuth, Mary, et al. "Synthetic Polymer Contamination In Global Drinking Water." Orb Media, 16 May 2017.

Quenqua, Douglas. "Microplastics Find Their Way Into Your Gut, a Pilot Study Finds." The New York Times, 22 Oct. 2018.

Royte, Elizabeth. "We Know Plastic Is Harming Marine Life. What About Us?" National Geographic, June 2018.

Wassener, Bettina. "Fish Ingesting Plastic Waste, Study Finds." The New York Times, 8 July 2011.

63 Climate Literacy: A Critical Step Toward Climate Stability

by Ella Shriner, 14, and Hannah Witscher, 15 (2017)

Climate change is a threat to every young person on our planet. It is vital that schools teach about the climate-caused tragedies that are occurring globally and how to combat climate injustice. Fortunately, some school districts are taking steps to ensure that this is done. In 2016 the Portland, Ore., school board unanimously passed a resolution supporting the teaching of climate justice.

In the New York Times article, "Setbacks Aside, Climate Change is Finding its Way into the World's Classroom," Alexander Leicht of Unesco states "[to slow climate change] we need an overall change of mind and a change of action that relates to everything that we think and do." Education can provide this essential change in perspective that will ultimately help the generations to come.

However, actions like Portland's are still relatively rare. There are too many cases of state legislatures, school districts and teachers actively denying the fact that climate change is real, or bowing to pressure from community members and corporations who value short-term profits over long-term climate stability.

Even when teachers and school districts want to teach the facts about climate change, many classroom resources discount the science behind climate change. Holt McDougal's textbook, "Modern World History," published in 2010, includes misleading statements questioning the legitimacy of the climate crisis such as, "not all scientists agree with the theory of the greenhouse effect." This statement falsely leads students to believe that there is not a wide scientific consensus about climate change.

Fossil fuel industry funding of curriculums also poses a huge obstacle to eliminating misinformation about climate change. Energy corporations are paying for materials to be developed that promote fossil fuel usage and production. In the Washington Post article, "Energy Industry Shapes Lessons in Public Schools," Kevin Sieff writes, "The industry aims to teach students about its contributions to local economies and counter criticism from environmental groups." These resources are often biased and factually incorrect.

Actions like Portland's demonstrate that schools can address climate change in the classroom. It is essential that cities around the nation follow their lead because we, as the future generation, deserve to know what we are facing and what we can do to fix this crisis that we did not create.

As Portland student Gaby Lemieux says, "Climate education is not a niche or a specialization, it is the minimum requirement for my generation to be successful in our changing world."

Sources

Gardiner, Beth. "Setbacks Aside, Climate Change Is Finding Its Way Into the World's Classrooms." The New York Times. The New York Times, 20 Apr. 2014. Web. 03 Apr. 2017.

Moore, Shasta Kearns. "Portland School Board Bans Climate Change-Denying Materials." Portland Tribune. N.p., 19 May 2016. Web. 2 Apr. 2017.

Sieff, Kevin. "Energy Industry Shapes Lessons in Public Schools." The Washington Post. WP Company, 02 June 2011. Web. 03 Apr. 2017.

64 Will the Future of American Manufacturing Be Printed?

by Ben Masters, 15 (2016)

Ever since Charles Hull invented the technology behind 3-D printing in the 1980s, the world of manufacturing has been one step behind its potential. This innovative technology can revolutionize American manufacturing into a customized process by enabling rapid prototyping, eliminating the extensive carbon footprint of manufacturing and decreasing the cost of custom consumer products. The solution to the wasteful and ecologically unsound practices of mass production in America is 3-D printing.

From my experiences in using 3-D printers in high school engineering classes, I have discovered how this revolutionary technology has the potential to change the world of manufacturing. 3-D printing uses raw materials to build objects layer by layer and reduces the amount of material used in manufacturing compared to traditional methods. According to the U.S. Department of Energy, subtractive manufacturing, the process of removing material from a block to create a product, can waste up to thirty pounds of material to create a one-pound product in some circumstances. However, 3-D printing uses 98 percent of the raw material used to make the final product in some methods. This technology has reduced the steps in the procedure of manufacturing and in turn reduces product costs.

3-D printing has enabled many in need to economically print customized prosthetic limbs. One in 2,000 children is born with an irregularity in an arm or hand. Unfortunately, until now children have rarely been given the opportunity to have a prosthetic arm because it costs about $40,000 to build one out of titanium. But with 3-D printing technology a family can economically print a prosthetic arm using about $20 of plastic filament. Although the pieces are not nearly as strong as titanium, they can be easily replaced or repaired when broken or outgrown. A prosthetic hand can be printed in about 20 hours and takes a few hours to construct using files from a free website, Thingiverse. This technology has made it possible for custom pieces to be manufactured at a reasonable price.

Although 3-D printing reduces the amount of raw materials used, it does use more electricity. The process of 3-D printing requires electricity to heat the extruder, the nozzle that melts the plastic filament, and ultimately build the object. Engineers are currently working to enable the use of 3-D printing while using less energy to reduce the carbon footprint of manufacturing.

The progressive technology behind 3-D printing is becoming more time efficient and economical. Siemens, the largest engineering company in Europe, envisions 3-D printing will become 50 percent cheaper and 400 percent faster in the next five years. The environmentally harmful methods of American manufacturing can be solved by the inventive technology of 3-D printing.

Sources

"How 3D Printers Work." Energy.gov. 19 June 2014. Web. 23 Mar. 2016.

Liffreing, Ilyse. "Beyond Plastic: 3-D Printing Goes Green." NBC New York. 17 Apr. 2015. Web. 23 Mar. 2016.

Mroz, Jacqueline. "Hand of a Superhero." The New York Times. 16 Feb. 2015. Web. 23 Mar. 2016.

Schull, Jon. "3-D Printers Put Limb Prosthetics for Kids in Reach." PBS. 23 Nov. 2015. Web. 23 Mar. 2016.

65 Driving: It's Going Out of Style

by Emma Chiu, 15 (2018)

As typical of an American high schooler, I recently underwent a teenage rite of passage: beginning to drive. My friends, who also have their driving permits, frequently joke with me about the woes of lane-changing, parallel parking and three-point turns as we prepare for our looming driver's license tests.

Yet we remain part of a dwindling majority. In 1976, nearly 87 percent of high school seniors held a driver's license. By 2016, this percentage dropped to under 72, a decrease that may correlate with a climbing dependence on parental or public transportation, a lack of car ownership, or simply not needing to drive anywhere.

Then add these declining rates to a rising innovation: autonomous cars. The introduction of effective autonomous cars could drastically reduce vehicular deaths, since 94 percent of traffic fatalities involve human error. Self-driving cars would eliminating the dangers of intoxicated driving, distracted driving or simply incompetent driving and render learning to drive unnecessary.

But, following the fatal Arizona crash between an autonomous Uber car and a pedestrian, Americans question the true safety of such technology. Company documents reveal that Uber's self-driving cars drove an average of only 13 miles before a human supervisor had to interfere to prevent a crash. In comparison, a study by Virginia Tech found that the average American driver crashes approximately once every 49,505 miles. Juxtaposed with the data of human drivers, Uber's autonomous cars appear laughably incompetent. Nevertheless, autonomous cars collectively travel about 113,636 miles per crash, indicating that they can and will be more reliable than humans.

Autonomous cars remain far from flawlessly navigating the roads, but we often fail to consider that developers designed our traffic regulations with humans—and human error—in mind. An entire network of self-driving cars would optimize traffic congestion and pollution by reducing the number of cars on the road. Consequently, regulations such as speed bumps and parking spaces may become restrictive rather than protective. To take full advantage of autonomous cars, we must prepare to rescind and replace longstanding laws.

As self-driving cars continue to improve, so does public reception of them. The percentage of Americans that distrust driverless cars decreased drastically from 74 percent in 2017 to 47 percent in 2018. If this downward trend continues, autonomous cars will soon be an accepted and integral part of society. Akin to penmanship and opera singing, human driving will soon be a practice of the past. And, given the potential security benefits and efficacy of autonomous cars, this is a future that we must accept—and even embrace.

Sources

Bahrampour, Tara. "Not Drinking or Driving, Teens Increasingly Put off Traditional Markers of Adulthood." The Washington Post, WP Company, 19 Sept. 2017.

Blanco, Myra. "Automated Vehicle Crash Rate Comparison Using Naturalistic Data." Virginia Tech Transportation Institute, Virginia Polytech Institute and State University, 8 Jan. 2016.

"Critical Reasons for Crashes Investigated in the National Motor Vehicle Crash Causation Survey." National Highway Traffic Safety Administration, Feb. 2015.

Giffi, Craig A. "A Reality Check on Advanced Vehicle Technologies." Deloitte Insights, Deloitte Insights, 5 Jan. 2018.

Wakabayashi, Daisuke. "Uber's Self-Driving Cars Were Struggling Before Arizona Crash." The New York Times, The New York Times, 23 March 2018.

66 A Prodigy for Your Progeny

by Kaiser Ke, 16 (2018)

In China, the competition is great and the opportunities are few. Children are faced with the burden of success the minute they are born. Before they are born, mothers are faced with the pressure of bearing the most well-advantaged offspring. In recent years, there has been an exponential rise in the number of couples who are opting to screen embryos during in vitro fertilization (IVF). Because of the financial burden, lack of facilities for, and social stigma of raising a handicapped child, Chinese parents are more willing to prioritize yousheng (which translates to "healthy birth") over the protection of an embryo.

One of the screening processes, known as preimplantation genetic diagnosis (PGD), is currently used to detect embryos with single gene mutations that could cause diseases and disabilities like Tay Sachs disease or cystic fibrosis. Chinese law prohibits selection of embryos based on anything else (for instance, selecting for male embryos is illegal). However, a whole new array of problems will develop as we achieve a greater understanding of what genes influence intelligence.

The trailblazer in this field is the Beijing Genomics Institute (BGI), which launched a project in 2012 to analyze the DNA of 2,000 of the world's smartest people. There are thousands of variants that influence mental abilities, but BGI aims to decipher the substantial genetic component of intelligence in the near future. While the study is purely academic, insight into the labyrinthine genetics of genius will define the future of genetic screenings; Pandora's box will be opened with no possibility for return.

Fertility clinics may go from advertising for "cancer-free babies" to promising "prodigy babies". The starting line for the rat race to the middle class will shift from family standing to predestined genetic design. PGD won't necessarily result in China mass-engineering super-citizens, but it will easily be misinterpreted by and desensitize result-driven consumers.

"Selecting for the smartest embryos" overemphasizes the hereditary facet of intelligence and glosses over the influence of nurture. Clinics cannot guarantee smarter babies, but eager couples will still flock to them nonetheless. In addition, even with PGD for simpler single gene mutations there is the risk of false positives. Now, couples might unknowingly dispose of perfectly healthy embryos in pursuit of a prodigy.

It is imperative that the Chinese government take proactive measures to oversee future PGD implementation. In addition to a moratorium so officials, scientists and consumers can deliberate, genetic counselors who are well-versed in bioethics need to lead a nationwide discussion on how far we are willing to let competition define us, literally. The human genome is indisputably the new frontier of exploration. However, unrestrained scientific ambition will move China forward before it is ready.

Sources

Cyranoski, David. "China's Embrace of Embryo Selection Raises Thorny Questions." Scientific American, Nature America, Inc, 16 Aug. 2017.

Eror, Aleks. "China Is Engineering Genius Babies." Vice, Vice Media, 15 March 2013.

Kolata, Gina. "Building a Better Human With Science? The Public Says, No Thanks." The New York Times, The New York Times, 26 July 2016.

Mukherjee, Siddhartha. The Gene: An Intimate History. Scribner, 2017.

Press, The Associated. "The Latest: Fertility Clinic's Embryo Tank Had Prior Trouble." The New York Times, The New York Times, 27 March 2018.

Sipp, Douglas, and Duanqing Pei. "Bioethics in China: No Wild East." Nature News, Nature Publishing Group, 13 July 2016.

Su, Baoqi, and Darryl R. J. Macer. "Chinese People's Attitudes Towards Genetic Diseases and Children With Handicaps." Eubios Ethics Institute, Institute of Biological Sciences, University of Tsukuba, 2003.

Yong, Ed. "Chinese Project Probes the Genetics of Genius." Nature News, Nature Publishing Group, 14 May 2013.

67 Paper or Plastic? How About a Paper ON Plastic!

by Melody Markert, 17 (2017)

As my mom opened the box containing our new Amazon Echo, I was shocked at the sheer amount of packaging that goes into shipping a nine-inch tall cylinder: It was enclosed in plastic, in a box, surrounded by Bubble Wrap, in yet another box. I should be glad that it keeps "Alexa" clean and protected, but I cannot overlook the amount of waste created. I recycled the cardboard, but the plastic? My neighborhood recycling plant only accepts plastic bottles. It does not have the facilities to break down the multilayered packaging economically. Instead, it went to the landfill, adding to the 14.4 million tons of plastic produced each year in America.

Granted, we have made progress over the years. Since 2005, United States companies have already avoided creating 1.5 billion pounds of packaging waste. Even so, reducing the amount of packaging is not enough. We must eliminate it entirely in order to see any large progress.

Zero waste stores have opened all across Europe in order to combat this issue. At Original Unverpackt, in Berlin, Germany, all of their products are out in the open, unobstructed by layers of plastic, paper or metal. Precycling removes trash before it is even created. Shoppers come in with sacks and totes buying local products while making conscious purchases.

Few places generate as much waste as grocery stores. We consistently see produce individually wrapped in plastic. But why is this necessary? For thousands of years, people bought goods fresh and in bulk—free of any sort of packaging. Bulk items are still around now, but their sections are dwarfed by aisles and aisles of unnecessary packaging. These small areas do not dominate stores and therefore have very little influence on our buying habits.

In America, a land full of supermarkets and large companies, it is more difficult to have zero waste and bulk markets because we want security and convenience. We pay for instant gratification rather than quality when we buy packaged food. If we want to reinvent grocery shopping, both the manufacturers and the consumers must take part.

Many large corporations such as Nestlé and WalMart have taken steps toward becoming more environmentally friendly, but lesser-known brands have made the most progress.

They have responded to the demands of consumers, eliminating excessive packaging and sourcing from local and organic farms. We need to continue this movement toward zero waste by encouraging consumers to change their way of life and look toward the future of healthy, sustainable living, rather than being content with harming our planet. Bring your own bags. Buy food in bulk. Shop zero-waste. Small changes are all it takes to make a difference that extends far beyond our own homes.

Sources

Ball, Aimee Lee. "The Anti-Packaging Movement." New York Times, 29 Nov. 2016. Accessed 25 Feb. 2017.

"The Facts." Recyclaholics, 2008. Accessed 5 Mar. 2017.

Johnson, Jim. "Food Industry Cuts Packaging Waste." Waste & Recycling News, vol. 16, no. 25, 18 Apr. 2011.

Physical and Mental Health

"He's 22 years old, a working man with a diploma, yet abled people always seem to have one inability: to see him as anything but a kid."

"Mental illness is a big deal."

"The discreet nature of vaping, and the game of cat and mouse that it inspires between teachers and students, is prompting a psychological shift."

68 U.S. Citizens Are Dying and We Can Save Them

by Eva Ferguson, 17 (2019)

I have a luxury that 27.3 million Americans don't: health insurance. Without it, my family would be hundreds of thousands of dollars in debt or I'd be dead.

In June of 2017 when my blood became dangerously acidic and my kidneys started to fail, I went to the ER. In June of 2017 when Alec Raeshawn Smith's blood also became dangerously acidic, he died before anyone could save him. Alec didn't have to die though; the insulin prescribed for his Type 1 diabetes could have saved him from the diabetic ketoacidosis that killed him. Alec, who had recently turned 26, could no longer afford his insulin because he was kicked off his mother's health insurance plan. Unable to afford the $1,300 a month cost for his insulin, he turned to rationing the insulin and died within one month of becoming uninsured. In the weeks after both of our incidents with acidosis, I went back to hanging out with friends and enjoying my summer.

Meanwhile, Alec's family was left making funeral arrangements.

There is only one way to prevent innocent people like Alec from dying: adopt national health insurance. With a single payer-program where the government subsidizes the cost of treatment, any and all citizens would be able to receive and afford any medically necessary treatment. Many fear that this program would cost an exorbitant amount of money and it is true that U.S. citizens would have to pay more in taxes to support it. However, US families, would save more money because they are no longer paying as much for health care costs like co-pays, premiums and deductibles. According to some studies, Senator Bernie Sanders's health care plan, which includes restrictions on drug markups, could save the U.S. government $2.1 trillion in the long run.

I have health insurance. Insurance that covers hundreds of thousands of dollars in medical bills, but that coverage runs out in nine years. My life after 26 is uncertain. Will I have a job that provides health benefits or will I be left hoping I won't get sick again? Health insurance can no longer be a political bargaining chip that gets thrown around as if people aren't dying without it. To make nationalized health insurance a reality, people like you need to decide health care is no longer a partisan issue; it's an American issue.

If we adopt a nationalized health care system, I will no longer live in fear for the day I might not be okay; I'll know my name will never be splashed across newspapers reminding politicians that they've killed one more citizen with their complacency.

Sources

Berchick, Edward. "Who Are the Uninsured?" The United States Census Bureau, 14 Sept. 2017.

Epstein, Randi Hutter, M.D., and Rachel Strodel. "Diabetes Patients at Risk From Rising Insulin Prices." The New York Times, 22 June 2018.

Haavik, Emily. "Mother Calls for Lower Insulin Prices in Wake of Son's Death." 10NEWS, 13 May 2018.

Stanley, Tiffany. "Life, Death and Insulin." The Washington Post Magazine, 7 Jan. 2019.

Stein, Jeff. "Does Bernie Sanders's Health Plan Cost $33 Trillion—or Save $2 Trillion?" The Washington Post, 31 July 2018.

69 Trivializing Mental Illness Makes Me Depressed

by Lola Byers-Ogle, 15 (2018)

"I swear, I'm so OCD," the girl says after neatly placing a bundle of colored pencils into a decorated pouch. I offer an awkward laugh, but all I can think about is my friend, whose OCD keeps him from going to school and hanging out with friends, or the article I read that says people with OCD are 10 times more likely than people without to commit suicide. How many times have you heard similar off-handed comments? "This class makes me depressed." "He's so psycho." Today, a girl described the weather as "bipolar."

These comments are thrown around frequently without any thought to the harm they might be doing. Even I've done it. Most of the time there's no malice, but comments like these, which trivialize serious illnesses, feed a society that stigmatizes the mentally ill, isolating them and making it impossible for them to live fulfilling lives.

Using mental illnesses like descriptive adjectives and not serious disorders is trivializing, and contributes to the stigmatization of those afflicted. NAMI (National Alliance on Mental Illness) estimates that 1 in 5 Americans suffers from a mental illness. Suicide is the 10th leading cause of death in the U.S.—claiming well over 41,000 lives a year. In simpler words, mental illness is a big deal; such a big deal the World Health Organization cites depression—just one of many mental illnesses—as the leading cause of disability. So why do we act like they're not by using them as descriptors or for cheap laughs?

Mental illness stigma leads to misunderstandings about the conditions and can create barriers to accessing treatment. In the New York Times piece "Alone With My Husband's Secret," Carolyn Ali writes of her husband's struggle with depression. Even after telling his wife, he asked to keep his condition a secret from his family members because of fear of their reaction. Ali says the experience also took a tremendous toll on her.

She wonders why these surprisingly common experiences are kept secret and why the stigma exists. This is just one story, but it underscores what experts say about stigma being a major cause of under-treatment.

Although there are many things that lead to the stigmatization of mental illness, and many reasons for treatment barriers, the trivializing of these conditions through jokes and minimization of the severity of the conditions is contributing to the exacerbation of the problem. It can be easily addressed through increased understanding of the words we use to describe experiences and ourselves. Recognizing how serious these disorders are and choosing not to use them as merely descriptors for an exaggerated situation is one small step to a society where stigma won't prevent those from getting the treatment that they need.

Sources

Ali, Carolyn. "Alone With My Husband's Secret." The New York Times, The New York Times, 1 Feb. 2018.

Hawkes, Nigel. "Stigma Is Leading to Under-Treatment of Mental Health Conditions, Says Leading Psychiatrist." The BMJ, British Medical Journal Publishing Group, 21 April 2016.

"Mental Health By The Numbers." NAMI: National Alliance on Mental Illness, 12 March 2018.

"Patients with OCD Are 10 Times More Likely to Commit Suicide." ScienceDaily, ScienceDaily, 19 July 2016.

Wilkerson, Abby L. "Should I Tell My Students I Have Depression?" The New York Times, The New York Times, 14 Dec. 2016.

70 How Ableism Lives On

by Hope Kurth, 17 (2016)

Five-star restaurant, four family members. A hostess sets down thick, leather menus in one, two, three places before proceeding to drop a flimsy half-piece of paper in front of my brother. He scrunches his eyebrows together and glares at my parents as if to say "not this again"—the kid-menu debacle that automatically ensues when you have Down syndrome. He's 22 years old, a working man with a diploma, yet abled people always seem to have one inability: to see him as anything but a kid.

Fortunately, the world is changing—with implementations like Best Buddies, Rosa's Law and the Americans With Disabilities Act. But a couple of things are keeping America from fully including and involving people with disabilities into everyday life naturally: society's colloquial language and the style of disability advocacy.

Thankfully, Spread the Word to End the Word and similar campaigns have attempted to mark words like "retarded" as taboo (however, 56 percent of Americans don't think it's offensive to call themselves the r-word, and 38 percent don't find a problem in calling their friends it either). But left in their wake are "boom-boom," "mental" and "slow." Of course, any well-intentioned person can forget and succumb to using these words—but if we ever want to see full integration, we have to let them go.

Some say that nitpicking words like "crazy" and "lame" will just start another political correctness battle, and that there is no easy way to eliminate them. But before deeming this challenge "too hard," think about how difficult it is for 48.9 million Americans to not only have a disability, but to be reminded of it in everyday conversations.

Another problem arises in the fact that two-thirds of people claim to be uncomfortable talking to people with disabilities because they don't know how to act politely around them. This awkward silence is too often filled with well-meaning (yet meaningless) statements like "You're God's special gift." But again, people who are uncomfortable around those with disabilities aren't usually out to discriminate. However, with the rise of politicians like Donald Trump, who "mocked" a reporter with arthrogryposis, more citizens are following the path to discriminatory speech.

Lastly, viral posts about those with disabilities have lately been deemed "inspiration porn," mainly for the reason that they've been used to inspire a retweet or a reblog, but no actual action. These posts make it seem as if the only purpose of those with disabilities is to inspire abled people—not to live a fulfilling life in the way they please.

Many of us possess good intentions about disabilities—but if we really want to solve ableism in America, we have to watch our patterns of speech (even jokes) and consider taking action instead of just hitting repost.

Sources

Haberman, Maggie. "Donald Trump Says His Mocking of New York Times Reporter Was Misread." The New York Times. The New York Times, 26 Nov. 2015. Web. 29 Mar. 2016.

Higgins, Karrie. "Dear Able Friends, I Am Not Your Inspiration Porn." The Huffington Post. TheHuffingtonPost.com, n.d. Web. 29 Mar. 2016.

"NSIP—Basic Facts: People with Disabilities." NSIP—Basic Facts: People with Disabilities. N.p., n.d. Web. 29 Mar. 2016.

"20 Amazing Disability Discrimination Statistics—BrandonGaille.com." Brandon-Gaillecom. N.p., n.d. Web. 29 Mar. 2016.

"Announcing 'The Shriver Report Snapshot: Insight Into Intellectual Disabilities in the 21st Century.'" Maria Shriver. N.p., n.d. Web. 25 Mar. 2016.

71 Vice for Vice

by Eugene Hong, 15 (2018)

Tobacco was, at one point, an American cultural cornerstone, as domestic as apple pie. That is, well, tobacco in the form of cigarettes. Now, because of vape pens—technology that delivers nicotine through heated oils—American youth are experiencing the rapid rebranding of our favorite vice. While vape companies such as Juul are capitalizing on the image of a sleeker, less carcinogenic way of getting buzzed, vaping is simply a method of concealing nicotine use, without eliminating any of its physiological consequences. The discreet nature of vaping and the game of cat and mouse that it inspires between teachers and students is prompting a psychological shift among youth that enables drug consumption, while masquerading as doing the opposite.

Joe Camel, the icon of tobacco conglomerate R.J. Reynolds, was executed in 1997, after nearly a decade of representing the Camel brand of cigarettes. The reasoning behind the federal government's decision to outlaw the swaggering camel was that he made smoking seem carefree and enticing to youth. Currently we are experiencing a more subtle version of the Joe Camel, in which vape pens such as Juul are reclaiming fun, risqué smoking. Not only do vapers have a nearly endless array of flavors to choose from, they also have apparatus that can disappear in a closed fist, according to a review of the Juul pen by NPR, which says owning a Juul is like a badge of honor. "Y'all this kid came into my 7th period to get a juul and we all started laughing when he left so the teacher was really confused," according to @hyphyybriannaa, quoted in the study.

A recent Times report on vaping attributes vaping partially to a decline in teenage cigarette smoking. While vaping is indeed helping teens move away from more carcinogenic forms of consuming nicotine, it also has the detrimental effect of making drug use seem more commonplace, cosmetic and convenient. After all, some brands of vaporizer can be charged in a laptop USB port, and concealed all day for undetectable puffing. Vaping might in fact just be hiding the harmful effect of drugs through a sleek image. In the National Institute on Drug Abuse study cited in the Times report, 51.8 percent of teens surveyed claimed that the substance inside vaporizers was "just liquid."

Does better technology make drug use permissive? No, but it certainly makes it easier. Vape pens are likely going to be short-lived in schools, which will make them only more appealing to youth. In order to truly lessen drug use, government and schools have to go after image, not just drugs themselves.

Sources

Chen, Angus. "Teenagers Embrace JUUL, Saying It's Discreet Enough To Vape In Class." NPR. 4 December 2017.

Elliot, Stuart. "Joe Camel, a Giant in Tobacco Marketing, Is Dead at 23." The New York Times. 11 July 1997.

Hoffman, Jan. "Marijuana and Vaping Are More Popular Than Cigarettes Among Teenagers." The New York Times. 14 December 2017.

72 Self-Care Alone Will Not Fix the System

by Walter Li, 18 (2019)

Mental health is entering the mainstream. The conversation has opened up as more high-profile individuals talk about their mental health struggles. As a mental health activist, I am thrilled at the momentum, yet I have reservations about the dominant focus of the conversation. Those reservations surfaced recently when I was posting a self-care tip about the value of journaling on the Instagram of my school's mental health club. Something felt off; telling people to journal felt like putting a band-aid on a broken arm.

Like my post, mainstream conversations oversimplify mental health. Self-care (meditation, mindfulness, and other self-help methods) have dominated current narratives. Media profiles of athletes or celebrities accessing treatment miss a crucial fact: treatment is still too expensive and stigmatized for the vast majority. Self-care tips are not enough. It is time for mainstream conversations to address how the mental health treatment system is fundamentally broken. It is time we talk about how to fix the system to offer accessible, comprehensive care for everyone.

The default in society is to deal with your mental illness alone: according to Mental Health America, 56.4 percent of adults struggling with a mental illness never get help. Imagine if 56.4 percent of adults with a broken arm never saw a doctor. How did we get here? After psychiatric asylums were closed in the United States, the goal was to replace them with a more supportive alternative. That alternative never came to fruition, meaning a comprehensive mental health system was never put in place.

The debate over solutions has some consensus: according to The New York Times Editorial Board, no one "wants to return to the era of 'insane asylums,' . . . Nor does anyone disagree that the 'system' that replaced them is a colossal failure." The core components of a working system include overall higher quality care with more treatment options and a greater bandwidth of medical programs including integrated and preventive care.

This system must be paired with insurance parity and a culture that makes accessing care clear, affordable, and de-stigmatized for everyone. According to Mental Health America, this new system must "support individuals at all stages of their recovery." Many people have promoted ideas for the exact details of this new system; however, these ideas cannot coalesce unless a discussion occurs in mainstream circles.

I do not write this editorial to say that self-care is less important. I write it to say that the status quo of the current mental health system must be challenged. This system is not working: it is too expensive, too inaccessible, and too stigmatized. We cannot go forward unless we carefully examine and alter mental health treatment. Now is the time to have that conversation.

Sources

The Editorial Board. "The Crazy Talk About Bringing Back Asylums." The New York Times, 2 June 2018.

"Mental Health in America—Access to Care Data." Mental Health America, 2019.

"Transforming the Mental Health System." Mental Health America, 2019.

73 A Psychedelic Cure?

by Reagan Briere, 16 (2017)

A South African crack cocaine addict walks into a clinic, disoriented and anxious. Thousands of miles away, in the sunlit suburbs of San Francisco, an author, mother of four, and former defense attorney reclines on a couch, preparing for what promises to be a change in perception. In New York City, a recent college graduate returns from an abridged European vacation to search for an answer to an impossible problem. Worlds away, the only factor that seems to unite these three individuals is a search—but for what?

All three—Thillen Naidoo, the author Ayelet Waldman, and Octavian Mihai—were dosed with a hallucinogenic drug as a last resort when cognitive behavioral therapy, medications, and other traditional remedies failed to alleviate their illnesses. All met with resounding success. Today, most classical hallucinogens are still heavily stigmatized due to their Schedule I status. However, recent evidence has begun to support the idea that the potential of hallucinogens to treat psychological disorders must be explored and legitimized.

Clinical trials at Johns Hopkins, N.Y.U., and other institutions have begun to illustrate the potential of hallucinogens to minimize the effects of depression, to help longtime smokers quit, to alleviate the symptoms of PTSD, and more. Many of these studies met with success rates of 80 percent or above when dealing with treatment-resistant patients. Tentative evidence has also begun to surface relating to the use of LSD "microdosing" to treat mood disorders and ibogaine to treat narcotics addictions.

Hallucinogenic drugs are unlikely to be employed as first resorts in the near future. However, the fact that over half of depression patients do not fully recover with an antidepressant medication and that anti-addiction drugs have success rates of less than 40 percent suggests that any potential solution to the world's battle with mental illness and addiction is sorely needed.

Some argue that the risks of hallucinogen use are too great to warrant their exploration as treatments for psychological disorders. However, hallucinogens do not have the same potential for addiction as alcohol, nicotine and opioids. In addition, hallucinogen persisting perception disorder—colloquially known as "flashbacks"—occurs in far lower frequencies than was originally thought in the 1970s and 1980s and is unlikely to occur in patients who take controlled doses of the hallucinogens in clinical settings.

Indeed, hallucinogens may be far safer than originally thought—not only physiologically, but also in the sense that their potential to treat high-risk disorders could save thousands of lives lost due to suicide, smoking-related cancers and overdoses each year.

Certainly, hallucinogens are no panacea. However, if their applications as treatments for psychological disorders are properly explored and their Schedule I status challenged, hallucinogenic drugs may prove to be the 21st century's next medical breakthrough.

Sources

Al-Harbi, Khalid S. "Treatment-Resistant Depression: Therapeutic Trends, Challenges, and Future Directions." Journal of Patient Preference and Adherence 6 (2012): 369–388. National Center for Biotechnology Information. Web. 23 Feb. 2017.

Hegarty, Stephanie. "Can a Hallucinogen from Africa Cure Addiction?" BBC News. The BBC, 3 Apr. 2012.

Hoffman, Jan. "A Dose of a Hallucinogen From a 'Magic Mushroom,' and Then Lasting Peace." The New York Times. The New York Times, 1 Dec. 2017. Web. 15 Feb. 2017.

Mithoefer, Michael C., et al. "The Safety and Efficacy of 3,4-Methylenedioxymethamphetamine-Assisted Psychotherapy in Subjects With Chronic, Treatment-Resistant Posttraumatic Stress Disorder: The First Randomized Controlled Pilot Study." Journal of Psychopharmacology 25.4 (2012): 439-452. Web. 24 Feb. 2017.

Phillip, Abby. "Hallucinogen in 'Magic Mushrooms' Might Have Helped Smokers Quit." The Washington Post. The Washington Post, 12 Sept. 2014. Web. 17 Feb. 2017.

Santella, Thomas. Understanding Drugs: Hallucinogens. New York: Chelsea House, 2012. Print.

Williams, Alex. "How LSD Saved One Woman's Marriage." The New York Times. The New York Times, 7 Jan. 2017. Web. 5 March 2017.

74 We Are the Generation of Self-Deprecation

by Faith Christiansen, 17 (2019)

We love self-deprecation.

After all, it is what fills the majority of our favorite jokes or humorous memes. We can't help but double-tap the post that states, "They said I could be anything! . . . So I became a disappointment" or "Who needs April Fools when your whole life is a joke?"

Self-deprecation is a major component of our conversations. Besides, would it sound right if I didn't put myself down every available chance? It's the "trendy" thing to be doing, as it fills every comedic sketch, video, and post on your feed. Social media pages are full of these constantly circulating messages that destroy self-image. One teen described his experience as such: "I come off as someone confident, but I suffer from such low self-esteem. Which defines my generation" (Levin). But, when did it become not only okay but expected for a class of teenagers to respond "same" when someone makes a suicide joke or says they are a failure? And where do we as a society draw the line? How are we supposed to differentiate between humor and someone's call for help?

Self-deprecation has become this generation's coping mechanism and is our new way of maintaining humility (Bellis). It's as if we have to validate taking care of ourselves. No wonder our mental health is deteriorating before our very eyes. According to *Time Magazine*, in a study, 91 percent of Gen Z adults feel symptoms of anxiety or depression, with 27 percent reporting their mental health as fair or poor (Ducharme). We make ourselves self-conscious when we don't have to, shame ourselves for things that don't matter and are overly critical in analyzing failures that could be simple mistakes. It is an epidemic, and we're all happily taking a part in it. It is self-sabotage and allows us to wallow in our problems rather than try to find solutions.

We are not only in a committed relationship with our misery but are in love with it. Suffering makes us happy (Sol). Our misery stems from the lack of self-confidence and grows into a flourishing constant state of mind. Each petal thriving from self-fulfilling prophecies hope for sympathy, self-generated stress, overeating, undereating, and critical self-evaluations (Luna). In a society that thrives off of being different, so many use that self-created pain to define their difference and create their individuality.

So be different, but more healthily. Know and advertise that it is okay to love yourself.

Use all of your quirks to define your success. Pay attention to how many times you put yourself down and stop doing it. Replace every negative thought with a compliment and become an advocate for self-love and self-worth.

Sources

Dahl, Melissa. "The 'Self-Esteem' Movement Is Over. Here's What's Taking Its Place." Fast Company, 14 June 2018.

Ducharme, Jamie. "More Than 90% of Generation Z Is Stressed Out." Time, 30 Oct. 2018.

Greenberg, Emma. "Opinion: Our Generation Needs to Stop Self Deprecating Out of Validation." The Eagle, 2 Nov. 2018.

Levin, Dan. "Generation Z: Who They Are, in Their Own Words." The New York Times, 22 March 2019.

Luna, Aletheia. "17 Habits of the Self-Destructive Person." LonerWolf, 9 March 2019.

Sol, Mateo. "Why Your Misery Makes You Happy." LonerWolf, 8 March 2019.

75 The Anguish of the Rich

by Yiqi Wang, 17 (2017)

China has experienced unprecedented economic growth in the past 30 years. A widely accepted positive correlation between happiness and wealth predicts that this growth should lead to higher life satisfaction, especially among the upper classes. Contrary to traditional understandings that equate increasing economic prosperity with increases in a nation's overall happiness, however, a recent paper on the paradox of Chinese progress draws an unusual conclusion:

In recent decades in China, life satisfaction declined dramatically at precisely the time of its unprecedented economic growth. More educated respondents, those in urban areas, and those with insufficient rest and leisure, are much less satisfied with their lives than the average.

The unhappiness of China's growing middle class illustrates the futility of equating material success with happiness. Long working hours and high workplace stress are usually the prerequisites for ascension to higher socio-economic status. Exposure to ever-higher standards for success triggers a persistent feeling of extreme pressure to succeed, and this phenomenon is especially conspicuous among the educated. Many find that their higher aspirations are combined with an increasing lack of security in the turbulent modern economy. A vicious cycle is formed, and those trapped within it begin experiencing feelings of anxiety and depression. An increase in the incidence of mental illness is a long-term manifestation of this phenomenon: China's psychiatric hospital admissions have increased by 183.21 percent from 2002 to 2012.

Karma Ura, president of The Centre for Bhutan Studies and GNH (Gross National Happiness) Research, has introduced a formula to gauge a nation's wealth according to the following criteria: access to a "ravishing environment," "vibrant health," "strong communal relationships" as well as "meaning in life and freedom to free time." If this formula is used as the benchmark for success, China's economic development has clearly been achieved at the price of many people's happiness.

In order to boost productivity, Deng Xiaoping converted the institutions of the highly-centralized planned economy to market institutions. This shift engendered a period of economic growth. While bringing economic prosperity to many, these largely-successful reforms also led to unchecked exploitation of land and natural resources, soaring average work intensity, rising income inequality and loss of communal beliefs. The legacy of reform includes severe environmental problems, a breakdown of social safety nets, and a conviction among the middle class that materialistic pleasure equals spiritual happiness. All these elements combined to create a sense of unhappiness among the bourgeoisie.

It is time that Chinese society prioritized mental health over economic success. The government should encourage this change by introducing GNH as a complement to GDP, placing more emphasis on improving people's well being and enacting policies that encourage a healthy work-life balance and a fair and secure environment for all.

Sources

Graham, Carol Shaojie Zhou, and Junyi Zhang. "Happiness and Health in China: The Paradox of Progress." Brookings Global Working Papers. Brookings Institution. 10 Jun. 2015. Web. 30 Mar. 2017.

Ryback, Timothy W. "The U.N. Happiness Project." The New York Times. 28 Mar. 2012. Web. 1 Apr. 2017.

Easterlin, Richard A., Fei Wang and Shun Wang. "Growth and Happiness in China, 1990-2015." World Happiness Report 2017. Web. 1 Apr. 2017.

Chow, Gregory C. "Economic Reform and Growth in China." Annals of Economics and Finance. 5 (2004): 93-118.

Arts, Culture, and Food

"I don't know if times have changed or movie writers have just forgotten what it felt like to be in high school."

"All I want is a culinary cultural revolution, is that too much to ask?"

"Unlike a 12-hour Netflix binge, reading statistically makes people happier."

76 Shakespeare: Friend, Not Foe

by Angela Chen, 15 (2019)

Now is the winter of our discontent. Or so Gloucester had said during the opening of "Richard III." But whereas Gloucester's winter has been made into a "glorious summer," this metaphorical winter of our discontent is far from over.

Why is it winter, then? Why, pray tell, am I in such discontent?

It is in more sorrow than in anger that I wear my heart upon my sleeve to say this. We, as a society, are treating the playwright who wrote these lines like the great villain of English literature—when he's far from it. For goodness sake.

Irrefutably, it's a rite of passage in high school, dissecting Shakespeare's long-drawn-out Elizabethan verses. These works all seem Greek to you, don't they? Why make sense of them on your own at all? And because of this, Shakespeare's reputation, good riddance, has seen better days.

Brevity is the soul of wit, said Polonius in "Hamlet," so I will make my voice concise. Have you even noticed eight Shakespearean phrases so far in this article already? That is how vital a presence he has even in contemporary English. When you "gossip," wait with "bated breath," feel "gloomy" or "bedazzled" or "dead as a doornail," you're revitalizing the Bard's memory. You "have not slept one wink" last night? Neither did Pisanio from "Cymbeline." Did you ever think Rose and Jack "star-crossed lovers"? So were Romeo and Juliet.

How can we defame a man who has changed the very face of language? How can we dismiss him as irrelevant, the original harnesser of the nuanced thing that is human emotion, just because we cannot understand him word-by-word?

It is time that we banish the notion of Shakespeare's works being highly academic, exclusive-to-scholars "scripture." Why? Because Shakespearean plays are built from emotion. Complaints on not being able to understand his words, in fact, trace all the way back to when his plays were first performed. So what if everyone cannot understand every word of Hamlet's dense, long-winding soliloquies? This is Shakespeare's very genius: to portray the raw anguish and internal strife of a young prince's lonely, grief-stricken heart. You need only follow the emotion, and the plays are lush with it.

As you read, acknowledge also the timelessness of this work. Motifs of racism and privilege in "Othello" and "The Merchant of Venice." Ambition and female agency in "Macbeth." Jealousy and unrequited love in "A Midsummer Night's Dream." Blackened vengeance in "Hamlet." These are ideas that transcend time, the things you relate to without having to understand every word on the page.

Shed your presumptions. Open your mind. Only then, pick up a play, and you will find within it a dish fit for gods.

Sources

Anderson, Hephzibah. "Culture—How Shakespeare Influences the Way We Speak Now." BBC News, BBC, 21 Oct. 2014.

Brown, Stephen. "Why Shakespeare? Because It's 2016." TedXStMaryCSSchool, 13 May 2016, Oshawa, 656 Taunton Road East.

Gaze, Christopher. "Shakespeare Is Everywhere." TedXVancouver, 21 Mar. 2012, Vancouver.

Shapiro, James. "Shakespeare in Modern English?" The New York Times, 7 Oct. 2015.

77 The Trouble With Teen Movies

by Olivia Newman, 18 (2018)

It's a Saturday evening. You're flipping through the television channels when you stumble upon the movie "She's All That." Or "Another Cinderella Story." Or "Freaky Friday." While each may have different characters, plot lines and messages, they are all classified as teen movies, which means they share one common feature: bullying.

The bullying that occurs in these films is usually of a specific type: The football player and his buddies see the nerd with his calculator in the hallway and shove him into a locker. The cheerleaders fill the chubby girl's locker with soda so that when she opens it, she gets drenched. The huge bodybuilder of a senior beats up the scrawny freshman who accidentally bumped his backpack.

I don't know if times have changed or movie writers have just forgotten what it felt like to be in high school, but in my four years of being a student, bullying has rarely been carried out in this manner. More often, it happens in whispers, through subtly closed off circles, through feigned compliments that turn into mocking giggles as soon as backs are turned. It happens over the internet: in group chats that exclude one specific person, in comments of "GORGEOUS!" under an Instagram post that the commenters definitely do not think is gorgeous. This cyberbullying is particularly prevalent in the lives of current teenagers, who have almost unlimited access to social media, and it "can have such a negative impact . . . [and] can do great harm to a whole peer group, or to school culture more generally." These more subtle types of harassment seem to be more prominent in a high school setting than physical attacks, and hurt much more.

Most teen movies fail to capture this kind of bullying accurately, and in this way contribute to an unrealistic view of high school life. Bullying can have very strong effects on teenagers, "causing depression and anxiety . . . disrupting [teenagers'] sleep, [and] causing gastrointestinal issues and headaches." If movies continue to portray bullying in the wrong way, not only may these symptoms be increased as teenagers begin to feel that their own experiences are invalid, but people will not be able to recognize true bullying behaviors. Kids are taught constantly in school not to be a bystander, but even the most noble of students cannot be expected to intervene when they don't realize that someone is being bullied. Teen movie writers need to take on the responsibility that comes with targeting the adolescent demographic, and complete research and focus groups to make sure that they are portraying one of the most common experiences in teenage life accurately. This, if nothing else, they owe to their viewers.

Sources

Klass, Perri. "In the Fight Against Bullying, a Glimmer of Hope." The New York Times, The New York Times, 22 Dec. 2017.

Strickland, Ashley. "Bullying Is a 'Serious Public Health Problem,' Experts Say." CNN, CNN, 21 June 2017.

78 A Change in the Menu

by Grace Silva, 15 (2019)

According to the Food and Agriculture Organization of the United Nations, an estimated two billion people eat bugs as part of their standard diet. That's nearly a quarter of the global population, and yet most countries in Europe and North America, despite the nutritional and environmental benefits, are fiercely reluctant to the idea of consuming bugs. So why should Westernized countries subscribe to the inclusion of bugs in their daily diet?

Eating bugs as a substitute for larger livestock could contribute substantially to a more sustainable world. Bugs have an efficient feed-to-product ratio and consume much less than traditional livestock per pound. To farm bugs, forests do not need to be cleared, fields do not need to be irrigated, and crops need not be sprayed with toxins and pesticides. According to an article written by the former manager of the Toronto Food Policy Council, Wayne Roberts, "Edible insects don't appear on any endangered species lists, and their sustainable use could help conserve other wildlife since the tactic may contribute to habitat protection."

The nutritional benefits of eating bugs are serviceable and can be instrumental in combating childhood mortality, and malnutrition rates. Monica Aiyeko of the Food and Agriculture department at Bondo University College has studied and published the effects of integrating native crickets into school meal programs in Kenya. Her studies have found that roughly 30% of Kenyan households are food insecure, leading to massive malnutrition amongst children, particularly under the age of 5. This is due to a lack of both macronutrients and micronutrients, including protein and zinc.

Incorporating bugs into school feeding programs could provide children with the necessary nutrients to prevent stunting. Overall, bugs and insects are incredibly nutritionally beneficial. The New York Times states that "Some 2,100 insect species worldwide have been identified as edible . . .

Their nutritional benefits, while varied across species, are substantial: high in energy yield, rich in essential amino acids and comparable and sometimes superior, per ounce, to beef, chicken, and pork in amounts of protein, omega-3 fats, iron, magnesium, calcium, and zinc."

The Western consensus is best stated by New York Times writer Ligaya Mishan: "Europeans, and by extension European settlers in North America, never had a bug-eating tradition. Indeed, we largely consider insects dirty and drawn to decay, signifiers and carriers of disease; we call them pests, a word whose Latin root means plague." This is a ridiculous stigma that we need to shake. The adoption of bugs into a normal diet would not be unlike the transition from raw fish being largely unaccepted in America, to sushi becoming a normal meal option.

All I want is a culinary cultural revolution, is that so much to ask?

Sources

Ilyashov, Alexandra. "How (and Why) to Cook With Bugs, According to Three Chefs." The New York Times, 10 Sept. 2018.

Mishan, Ligaya. "Why Aren't We Eating More Insects?" The New York Times. 7 Sept., 2018.

Münke-Svendsen, Christopher and Kipkoech Carolyne, John Kinyuru, Monica Ayieko, Anja Homan and Nanna Roos. "Technical Brief #5: Nutritional Properties of Insects for Food in Kenya." University of Copenhagen, 2017.

Roberts, Wayne. "Eating Insects: Waiter, There's No Fly in My Soup." Alternatives Journal, vol. 34, no. 1, Jan.-Feb. 2008, p. 8+. Academic OneFile, Accessed 6 Mar. 2019.

Sheraton, Mimi. "Eating Raw Fish: The Dangers." The New York Times, 30 Sept. 1981.

79 Let Children of Color Be Characters, Too

by Sandra Chen, 16 (2018)

Two facts about me: I am Chinese American, and I am a writer. I only recently recognized the connection between these two facets of myself—or rather, the lack of one: in all of my stories since childhood, I had never written about a Chinese American character. The reason? I'd never really read about one either.

The lack of ethnic representation in children's literature is stark. According to the publisher Lee & Low, only about 10 percent of children's books published in the last two decades contain diverse themes. Meanwhile, roughly 80 percent of people involved in children's literature—authors, illustrators, editors, publishers, etc.—are white. When people of color constitute roughly 39 percent of the current U.S. population, these numbers convey a serious problem. It has been said that books act as mirrors, allowing readers to reflect on their own identities. Children of color are deprived of the opportunity to truly see themselves in the pages they read, thus made to understand that they can never be the protagonists of their own stories.

Too often, multicultural books are pushed aside because they can't connect with the majority of white readers. But to make such an argument when nonhuman characters are so popular in children's literature is to suggest that white children have more in common with animals than other children. Moreover, research has continuously shown that reading facilitates empathy and understanding. A study conducted by Laurel Hartmann specifically found that multicultural picture books "helped encourage the students to search for similarities between their own lives and the lives of members of diverse cultures around the world." Thus, representative books may be just as important for white children as for children of color.

In recent years, more and more attention has been brought to this issue. In 2014, an online campaign under the hashtag #WeNeedDiverseBooks turned into a nonprofit organization that advocates for diversity in children's literature. Independent publishers such as Lee & Low Books, Arte-Publico Press' Piñata Imprint, and Just Us Books have introduced more diverse characters into print. It is up to us to support these efforts to ensure that children of color have a chance to see themselves and be seen, to remember that their stories are just as real, valid and deserving. It is up to us to buy diverse books from local bookstores, contact school libraries to ask for more inclusive selections, and promote minority writers who are representing their communities.

And as a young minority writer myself, I am learning to find my voice and to speak out for all those who have lost their own. In doing so, I hope that the writers of the next generation will never learn to silence their heritage as I did.

Sources

Hartmann, Laurel K. "Using Multicultural Literature in the Classroom to Encourage Tolerance and Respect." MS Thesis. Rowan University, 2011.

Low, Jason. "Where is the Diversity in Publishing? The 2015 Diversity Baseline Survey Results." Lee & Low Books. 26 Jan. 2016.

Myers, Christopher. "The Apartheid of Children's Literature." The New York Times. 15 Mar. 2014.

Perez, Domino Renee. "Characters in Children's Books Are Almost Always White, and It's a Big Problem." The Washington Post. 8 Dec. 2014.

Slater, Dashka. "The Uncomfortable Truth About Children's Books." Mother Jones. 10 Sep. 2016.

80 A Massacre of Art

by Josh C. (2015)

From Bob Marley to The Black Keys, Bon Iver to Flume, and all the well-known to underground artists in between, there's a simple requisite for admission into my musical palette: a song's ability to communicate, provoke thought, and capture emotion. As a music lover, I've spent many hours expanding my iTunes library, and have been able to find obvious talent throughout almost the entire spectrum of genre.

Except pop.

Whether it's Ryan Seacrest's Top-40 or a hit-music station's playlist, it's hard to extract even a basic appreciation for this artless genre. "Blah Blah Blah" by Ke$ha, Miley Cyrus's "FU", and JuicyJ's "Bandz a Make Her Dance", are just a few tunes that make pop especially hard to respect . . . Not only is it bad music, it is bad for music, as it degrades the uniquely expressive art form that has left entire audiences intoxicated with emotion (and not because Justin Bieber just took his shirt off while singing in falsetto).

It's easy to pinpoint lacking musical elements of pop: lyrically it is shallow, vocally it's mediocre, and instrumentally it's bland. Pitbull's lyric, "mami got an ass like a donkey with a monkey/Look like King Kong" pretty much sums up the theme of lyrical senselessness. Vocal incompetence is exposed in pitchy live performances, which critic Jon Caramanica says, "reflect . . . the utter dearth of viable contemporary . . . pop stars." And finally, its repetition of overused rhythms and cheesy melodies account for the dreary instrumentals.

However, Lady Gaga doesn't have 44.7 million Twitter followers for nothing, and there's a reason Taylor Swift has 4 number-one albums . . . but what is it? Surprisingly, there's a simple answer– the exposure effect. Explained in research out of Gettysburg College, one's likelihood of enjoyment greatly increases when exposure to the stimulus increases. Upon discussing this reality in the music industry, Tom Barnes explains that, "repeated exposure is a much more surefire way of getting the general public to like a song than writing one that suits their taste." He says that this, combined with the reality of payola (a record label's illegal bribing for broadcasting of their song), create almost a perfect pedestal for the acceptance of pop music, however bad it is.

It is disappointing that future generations will be raised on metaphors comparing a donkey/monkey hybrid to a woman's rear end, rather than a properly poetic one in, say, John Mayer's intro to "Bold As Love." It is even more disappointing that inspiration for popularized music has become profit (as Drake says, "as long as the outcome is income"), rather than expression. But this doesn't have to continue— all it takes is a conscious listener.

You can be that listener.

Sources

Barnes, Tom. "How The Music Industry Is Brainwashing You to Like Bad Pop Songs." Mic. N.p., 04 Aug. 2014. Web. 05 Mar. 2015.

Bornstein, Robert F., and Paul R. D'Agastino. "Stimulus Recognition and the Mere Exposure Effect." Journal of Personality and Social Psychology 63 (1992): n. pag. Print.

Caramanica, Jon. "Not Exactly Brilliant, but at Least the Colors Are." The New York Times. The New York Times, 01 Feb. 2015. Web. 05 Mar. 2015.

Caufield, Keith. "Taylor Swift Collects Fourth No. 1 Album, 'Now 52' Debuts at No. 2." Billboard. N.p., 5 Nov. 2014. Web. 05 Mar. 2015.

"'I Know You Want Me (Calle Ocho)' Lyrics." PITBULL LYRICS. N.p., n.d. Web. 05 Mar. 2015. http://www.azlyrics.com/lyrics/pitbull/iknowyouwantmecalleocho.html

81 There Is No Happily Ever After Without Once Upon a Time

by Bridget O'Leary, 17 (2017)

It is no secret that Hollywood is dominated by cisgender, heterosexual, conventionally attractive white people. Members of minority groups struggle to find accurate representation in films, clinging tightly to even the smallest examples of representation. This lack of diversity is particularly damaging to young children, whose perception of the world is warped to fit a narrative where only a certain type of person gets to have a happily ever after.

In 2015, only 22 out of 126 released films featured a character that was part of the L.G.B.T.Q.+ community. Some people argue that because there are more cis-heterosexuals in real life, there should be more cis-heterosexuals in films. By this logic, the number of cis-heterosexual characters in individual films should exceed L.G.B.T.Q. characters. The lack of L.G.B.T.Q.+ characters in over 100 films creates entire universes where L.G.B.T.Q.+ people are seemingly nonexistent, a statistic that does not mirror reality in the slightest.

Children especially need to see L.G.B.T.Q.+ characters, and yet their demographic is the one that is most denied access to films with accurate representation. Unfortunately, many people consider same-sex relationships to be too mature for children. Because of this, impressionable young people are prevented from watching films that could help them to better understand themselves and to accept the people around them.

This also prevents L.G.B.T.Q.+ people and relationships from becoming normalized. If children are not exposed to the L.G.B.T.Q.+ community until later on in life, they will learn to treat it as something new and different as adults. By showing them films with diverse casts of characters, children will recognize that L.G.B.T.Q.+ people are a part of everyday life and that they "have a right to . . . their happily ever after, too." Normalizing

L.G.B.T.Q.+ identities will also normalize their inclusion in films and other media outlets, because the people making those films will be so used to a world of L.G.B.T.Q.+ people that to not include them would be unthinkable.

Film companies argue that parents would not allow their children to see films with L.G.B.T.Q.+ characters in them, making diversity and inclusivity bad for business. Though there are certainly people who would boycott films on this basis, there are also many parents who would be thrilled to see their children introduced to that kind of diversity at such a young age. Many L.G.B.T.Q.+ adults would watch the films as well, because they want to experience the representation they were denied as a child.

Representation in any type of media is important, but L.G.B.T.Q.+ visibility in children's films is of particular significance. It represents another step on the long road to equality and a shift in the mind-set of an entire generation.

Sources

Bahr, Lindsey. "Are 'Gay Moments' in 'Beauty' and 'Power Rangers' Progress?" Associated Press. 24 Mar 2017. Web.

"LGBT Community Faces 'Invisible' Hollywood Summer Movie Season." The New York Times. 25 May 2017. Web.

"Overview of Findings." GLAAD. 02 May 2016.

82 The Integrity of Pineapple Pizza

by Sarah Celestin, 16 (2019)

For many years those who enjoy pineapple on their pizza have faced ridicule. Many people strongly disagree with the combination pineapple and pizza, and while it is understood that not all opinions are always completely agreed on, the perspectives of pineapple pizza eaters have been disrespected for far too long. The outright disgust expressed by non-pineapple pizza eaters is a contradiction to some of the world's favorite foods. For centuries various fruits, such as mango and watermelon, have been topped with salt and chili mixes, but the reaction to the list of concoctions previously stated do not even begin to compare to the reactions to pineapple pizza. Salted caramel, kettle corn, chocolate covered pretzels, peanut butter and jelly sandwiches: these are all snacks that are widely loved, but carry the same flavor profiles as pineapple pizza. So why is pineapple pizza so hated?

Scientifically pineapple pizza stimulates two major areas of the tongue that are responsible for flavor—sweet and savory. Our bodies naturally crave sweetness because it signals calorie intake, and saltiness because sodium is necessary for certain everyday bodily functions. The flavors of pineapple and pizza work so well together because it tackles two instinctive cravings at once. Pineapple is also a great source of vitamin c and magnesium. Vitamin c is essential for the growth, development and the production of collagen, and magnesium helps with bone formation and calcium absorption. Pineapples create a new dynamic for boring everyday pizza by adding a tropical twist *and* increasing its nutritional value.

Pineapple pizza eaters are not looking for validation, they are just looking for respect. They refuse to be belittled for their choices any longer. The president of Iceland, Gudni Thorlacius Johannesson, once said that should he be able to pass laws, he would like to ban pineapple as a pizza topping. Is the choice of having pineapple on pizza that bad to the point where a president would make it illegal if he had the ability to? Remarks like this revile the choices of all pineapple eaters everywhere. Let's ask ourselves, Is it fair to judge what a person decides to indulge? Is it fair to make a person feel bad because they enjoy something you may not? Put yourself in the position of a pineapple-pizza eater before you decide to make a face or a snarky remark about the harmless decision of enjoying a slice of pineapple pizza.

Sources

Behm, Mackenzie. "The Scientific Reason Why Pineapples Belong on Pizza." Spoon University, 28 April 2017.

Pogrebin, Robin. "Pineapple Pizza Tests Limits of Presidential Power in Iceland." The New York Times, 22 Feb. 2017.

83 To Read or Not to Read?

by Anna Brooke May (2015)

George R.R. Martin claimed "A reader lives a thousand lives before he dies . . . The man who never reads only lives one." Unfortunately, reading for fun has become a cultural anomaly for American teenagers because it requires imagination, patience, and focus. By emphasizing the importance of independent reading, academic institutions foster the aforementioned skills that are under attack by fast-paced media culture.

The time constraint plaguing America's youth, due to the hours of extracurricular activities that occupy competitive student's lives, is partially to blame. Despite the increasing pressure on students to succeed academically, in 2014 only 31% of students ages 6-17 claimed to read daily (Rich). Not only is this detrimental to student's reading comprehension skills, but it also undermines the well-rounded student and justifies shortcut culture.

A common misconception is that the writer does all of the creating. Unlike movies that define every visual on a silver screen, literature allows the reader to envision his own interpretation of the story. When students are reading, they are not only practicing analytical skills, but they are also exercising the part of the brain that thinks independently. Promoting this unhindered thinking encourages a generation of innovative thinkers who will inevitably break barriers in their chosen field.

Unlike a twelve-hour Netflix binge, reading statistically makes people happier. The Bookseller Media Group reports that 20% of people who read for only thirty minutes per week admit greater satisfaction with their lives. So, by sacrificing one episode of Friends, you are 21% less likely to feel depressed and 10% more likely to have improved self-esteem (Shaffi).

In consideration of the wisdom of Mr. Martin, let's ask what constitutes a full life: World travels? Prestigious education? Wild adventures? Reading is so vital for the developing mind because it allows exploration of places, cultures, and events that would be foreign to us otherwise. Pat Scales argues that if children are exposed to stories, "they will become kinder and gentler toward those . . . in another part of the nation or world."

Because literature is so expansive, every book represents a novel universe that any reader will yearn to explore if he or she will invest the time. The gratification in finishing a book is so great, and the benefits so numerous, that educational institutions have nothing to lose by promoting extracurricular reading. Consequently, if America is serious about bringing up a more cultured generation, they should heed the philosophy of great American writer Dr. Theodore Seuss Geisel: "The more that you read, the more things you know. The more that you learn, the more places you'll go."

Sources

Martin, George R. R. A Dance with Dragons. New York: Bantam, 2011. Print.

Rich, Motoko. "Study Finds Reading to Children of All Ages Grooms Them to Read More on Their Own." New York Times 8 Jan. 2015: A16(L).General OneFile. Web. 7 Mar. 2015.

Scales, Pat. "On the street where I lived." Booklist 1 Nov. 2014: S40. General OneFile. Web. 7 Mar. 2015.

Seuss. I Can Read with My Eyes Shut. New York: Beginner, 1978. Print.

Shaffi, Sarah. "Reading makes you happier." The Bookseller 6 Feb. 2015: 16. General OneFile. Web. 7 Mar. 2015.

Sports and Gaming

"Until I lost several months of my life, I had not wanted to believe that video game addiction was real."

"It's sad, but it is time for tackle football to go."

"It brings to mind the flowing hair of golden retrievers and leaping hippies, not serious athletics."

84 Confronting Toxicity in Gaming: Going Beyond 'Mute'

by Tony Xiao, 15 (2019)

The recent spate of white nationalist violence has raised concerns about the role online platforms play in the radicalization of attackers. Analysts have noted the disturbing tendency of YouTube algorithms to lead users to extreme content. Others have bemoaned social media's role in the viral propagation of racially charged fake news. While internet companies are finally starting to respond (Facebook recently announced a ban on white nationalist content), there remains one lesser-mentioned vehicle for racial desensitization: online gaming.

I don't mean the violent content of online games. Violent content is a boogeyman over-hyped by pundits. I'm referring to the racist, anti-Semitic way gamers are indoctrinated to speak to each other in the depersonalized realm of online competition. The ritual, similar to fraternity hazing, happens something like this:

A new gamer, let's call him "Joe," joins a game of Minecraft, a pixelated world-building game with 100 million active players. Joe tells his teammates he's new to the game. When he drags his team down, his teammates begin to trash-talk him, firing racist, sexist and homophobic insults his way. After this bout of shaming, Joe builds his skill level. Months later, Joe queues up for a game, and sees a novice assigned to his team. After finally losing because of his teammate's poor skills, he insults the player using the same script he had been abused by months earlier. Joe is now a part of the toxic cycle.

Prominent gaming companies like Blizzard and Riot have started creating systems to combat the hate speech rampant in gaming communities. Certain platforms temporarily mute players after instances of racist profanity. But in most cases, these measures are perfunctory, amounting to a slap on the wrist. Players evade censors easily by omitting letters or adding numerals to ethnic slurs written in game chats.

Gaming companies need to step up their efforts by punishing abusive players with meaningful competitive penalties. E-sports can look to an obvious model: real-world sports. Violence on the hockey rink takes a player off the ice for critical game time. Tennis players can be docked points, games or even matches for verbal abuse. In the world of e-sports, a similar dynamic might include lower maximum health, longer skill cool-down periods, or other handicaps. Unless penalties come down in a manner meaningful to players, hate speech will continue to flourish.

Players should self-monitor and realize that the racially-charged insults they hurl have real-world consequences. But, knowing the culture as it exists now, perhaps that ship has sailed. Such a deeply rooted problem calls for an strong, top-down approach. It's time the gaming industry understood that it has a responsibility to stem the spread of hate on its platforms.

Sources

Moore, Bo. "Major Game Companies Are Teaming Up to Combat Toxicity in Gaming." PC Gamer, 22 March 2018.

Schiesel, Seth. "The Real Problem With Video Games." The New York Times, 13 March 2018.

Weill, Kelly. "How YouTube Built a Radicalization Machine for the Far-Right." The Daily Beast, 17 Dec. 2018.

85 Why I, a High School Football Player, Want to See Tackle Football Taken Away

by Keegan Lindell, 17 (2019)

You feel a cool drop of sweat slide down your spine, sparking chills throughout your body. Your eyes dart back and forth in hopes of spotting the kamikaze player coming in. Shoulder to shoulder, you are a shield for the returner; however, a man disguised as a bomb sails through a gap five yards away and strikes head first into the teammate next to you. With a loud disturbing crack, anger, hatred, fear, and desperation fill your body. Paler than an albino, he rises with a stumble and it's apparent that fear has overtaken his eyes along with a look of confusion. Knowing he isn't all right, you insist he gets off the field; nevertheless, he needs to prove his manhood and forces himself back into the huddle.

Sadly, this is the reality of tackle football.

Excitement, brotherhood, life lessons are all extraordinary things that the game brings to your life; however, it brings brain diseases, concussions, and lifelong ripple effects as well. With the knowledge that our brain doesn't stop developing until our mid-twenties, the last thing you want to do is injure it. According to the Nida Blog Team article, teens and children are at a higher risk for concussions because the "brain's nerve fibers can be torn apart more easily." Why expose our nation's future to potential brain damage?

Human anatomy is not built for football. Humans lack a "safety belt" for the brain and instead have protective fluid that can send the brain flying into your skull wall and severely bruise it. Meanwhile, a woodpecker that slams its beak into a tree can absorb the force through its beak and a muscle that wraps around the brain so it can't collide into the skull. Since humans lack this, we are prone to concussions. According to the New York Times, a former NFL player is "three to four times more likely" to develop "brain diseases, including Alzheimer's, Parkinson's, and amyotrophic lateral sclerosis."

Instead of being oblivious to these problems, we should be concerned about the symptoms of football and take action.

At such a vital point in my developmental life. I am ripped apart between my love of the game and my growing realization that tackle football is not safe. As an avid football player since the fourth grade, I have reluctantly come to the conclusion that if I have future sons, they will not play tackle football. We need to make the wiser choice and lead ourselves into a safer future by removing one of my greatest passions. It's sad, but it is time for tackle football to go.

Sources

Gonchar, Michael. "If Football Is So Dangerous to Players, Should We Be Watching It?" The New York Times, 13 Sept. 2012.

The NIDA Blog Team. "Traumatic Brain Injury, Drug Addiction, and the Developing Teen Brain." National Institute on Drug Abuse for Teens, 19 Mar. 2015.

86 Concussion Hysteria

by Aidan Donnelly, 17 (2016)

Concussions are undoubtedly a serious issue in contact sports and the safety protocol regarding concussions should and is being improved. However, today when a coach, teammate or parent asks if you've had concussions, it's like admitting you have the plague. After expressing their pity for your perilous condition, many people question your decision to play contact sports and whether you understand the "long term effects." Suddenly, you're not only crippled but are uneducated about your terrible affliction and deserve a lecture on your decision to participate in the sports you love.

Ironically, the concussed community is extremely knowledgeable on the effects of concussions and exactly what has happened to our brain. We've heard speeches from the doctors, parents and concerned relatives, and even our beloved ESPN has reported tirelessly on the negative effects of concussions. The last thing we need or want is another speech about why we should take our injuries seriously, as if we've ignored the information that has been constantly presented to us.

The constant reiteration and possible dramatization of concussions' damage has caused the vilification of contact sports, particularly football. A New York Times article titled "Youth Tackle Program Is Being Eliminated in a Football Hotbed" by Ben Kelson covers how the town of Marshall, Texas, traditionally a town full of football talent, has disbanded its Pee Wee football program because of concern for the lasting effects of head trauma.

Despite the overwhelming concern from parents and communities about concussions in contact sports, some scientists are preaching a message of calmness when discussing the current concussion issue. A STAT article titled "The Sky Is Not Falling: Congress Looks at the Science of Concussions" by Dylan Scott, highlights Dr. David Cifu's comments during a congressional panel meant to review the dangers of concussions. Dr. Cifu stated, “The sky is not falling.” Later adding, “The advances we’ve made in treatment are significant. I would suggest that it’s never been safer to have a concussion.” Throughout the panel, Dr. Cifu claimed that people where overreacting to concussions and prematurely pulling athletes from sports.

Dr. Cifu gives me hope that people can begin to look at concussions rationally. Rather than fearing concussions, people should be well educated on them and aware of how well concussions are dealt with medically. The process of reducing concussions and their effects is still maturing but is making rapid progress. By taking a serious but fearless approach, we can balance our society’s love of contact sports with the safety and longevity of our athletes.

Sources

“‘The Sky Is Not Falling’: Congress Looks at Science of Concussions. STAT.

“Youth Tackle Program Is Being Eliminated in a Football Hotbed.” The New York Times.

87 This Is Not a Game

by Ben C., 16 (2016)

Until I lost several months of my life, I had not wanted to believe that video game addiction was real. It took me two months at a wilderness camp to recover and now a lifetime in which I'll have to carefully consider my media usage. Gaming dominated every hour of my life. Even when my teachers, parents and friends actively tried to intervene, I couldn't stop. I used exciting adventures and action-filled shooters to escape from a dull-by-contrast world. I was absolutely hooked.

Gaming addiction is being increasingly recognized by medical professionals as a 'process addiction' akin to gambling. Scans of the pleasure centers of brains of game addicts 'light up' in the same ways as of those addicted to cocaine or heroin. Video games are designed to be—by the gaming industry—a very active experience that draws in and immerses a player in a world they are reluctant to leave.

China has government-sponsored camps to treat young addicts. It recognizes and understands this problem. America does not. Here, gaming addiction gets scant media coverage, if any. This is a serious mistake with such a large population at risk. 81 percent of U.S. households own a gaming device. In an Iowa State University study of gamers, nine percent showed signs of gaming addiction, indicating that three million young people are at risk.

Society has mechanisms to help those who cannot help themselves. Families stage interventions, legislators ban sales of drugs, and doctors provide emergency services without regard to insurance. Those who need outside intervention and support deserve the same assistance as a burn victim who can't bandage themselves. The Diagnostic and Statistical Manual of Mental Disorders does not list compulsive gaming as a clinical disorder, suggesting that it might be caused by unrelated disorders like depression or ADHD and saying it 'needs further study'. Completely ridiculous. As I know all too well, gaming addiction dominates a person's life, provides an escape, and causes withdrawal just like a "real" addiction. It must be treated like one, too. To start, the American Psychiatric Association should add gaming addiction into the DSM as a clinical disorder. In addition, the government should both sponsor campaigns that educate the general public and add video game addiction to the topics covered by health and human development courses in high schools. Based on my experience, the best kinds of treatment facilities are those that place kids in an environment where they have the opportunity for self-reflection and healing, sans devices.

If this problem remains unrecognized, we may soon have a 'lost generation' of teenagers and adults whose entire lives are consumed by video game and media addiction.

Sources

Brody, Jane E. "Screen Addiction Is Taking a Toll on Children." New York Times 6 July 2015: n. pag. Print.

Iowa State University. ISU's Gentile contributes to study identifying risks, consequences of videogame addiction. Ames: ISU, 16 Jan. 2011. Print.

Lenhart, Amanda. "Teens, Social Media & Technology Overview 2015." Pew Research Center (2015): n. pag. Print.

Rich, Michael, MD. Personal interview. Feb. 2015.

Sarkis, Stephanie, Ph.D. "Internet Gaming Disorder in DSM-5." Psychology Today. Sussex, 18 July 2014. Web. 16 Mar. 2016.

88 The Future Disintegration of American Democracy Through Athletics

by Julianne Yu, 16 (2017)

In 2012, Allen Independent School District in Texas spent $60 million on a new football stadium, at the time, the most expensive high school stadium ever. In fact, The New York Times reports that it has nearly the same capacity as Madison Square Garden.

Now, McKinney Independent School District, adjacent to Allen I.S.D., is building a rival stadium for nearly $70 million. That's the equivalent of providing school lunch to all of the 24,500 students in McKinney every day for six years.

This is a remarkable misappropriation of money in a state that chronically underfunds education. As of last year, not only did Texas rank 43rd in the nation for education, it ranked 49th in per pupil spending. Nationally, the U.S. spent an average of $11,667 per student whereas Texas fell behind at $7,957 per student. But it's not only Texas whose obsession with sports is ripping at the seams of our educational system and, consequently, our democracy.

A democracy forming without the proper education is doomed to crumble. Education is the key in arming the electorate with the information necessary to consider candidates, yet superfluous spending toward athletics is hindering the way our society is learning and voting. Paving the path toward a strong democracy, not a sharply divided one, begins and ends with education. Shifting the focus from athletics to academics, from the playing field to the classroom, is the way to uphold our trembling nation. As Richard D. Kahlenberg and Clifford Janey explain, "The Founders saw education as the safeguard of America's system of self-governance. Educating common people was the answer to the oligarchs who said the average citizen could not be trusted to choose leaders wisely." But with more than two-thirds of Americans unable to name all three branches of government, I can't help but ponder: Is this the America that our founders had hoped for?

Defunding sports is absurd. It is just as vital to have an active society as it is to have an educated one. But athletics cannot be the top priority when the U.S. is ranked so low in education. The Pew Research Center reports that the U.S. is currently 38th out of 71 developed and developing countries in math, and 24th in science. We are one of the wealthiest countries in the world, but our school funds are going down the wrong drain. Author Marguerite Roza "found that one high school was spending $328 a student for math instruction and more than four times that much for cheerleading—$1,348 a cheerleader."

Spend tax money wisely; invest more in education; prioritize academics over athletics. And, who knows? Maybe if we spent $60 million on libraries instead of sports stadiums, students would understand that their society values education. And they would vote accordingly.

Sources

Anderson, Lindsey. "Texas Falls to 43 in National Education Ranking." El Paso Times. 11 Jan. 2016.

DeSilver, Drew. "U.S. Students' Academic Achievement Still Lags That of Their Peers in Many Other Countries." Pew Research Center. 15 Feb. 2017.

Gerber, Marisa. "After Texas High School Builds $60-million Stadium, Rival District Plans One for Nearly $70 Million." Los Angeles Times. 17 Sept. 2016.

"McKinney ISD Meal Prices for the 2016-17 School Year." McKinney ISD. N.d.

McPhate, Mike. "That's Right, $63 Million for a Football Stadium . . . for High Schoolers." The New York Times. 11 May 2016.

Richard D. Kahlenberg and Clifford Janey. "Is Trump's Victory the Jump-Start Civics Education Needed?" The Atlantic. 10 Nov. 2016.

Ripley, Amanda. "The Case Against High-School Sports." The Atlantic. 19 Feb. 2014.

89 It's Time for America to Start Feeling the Love for Ultimate Frisbee

by Alex Kucich, 17 (2016)

There is something misleadingly whimsical about the word "frisbee." It brings to mind the flowing hair of golden retrievers and leaping hippies, not serious athletics. However, it is time Americans realized that frisbee has become something far more formidable and new. Yes, Ultimate Frisbee has recently burgeoned into a fiercely competitive, physically demanding and increasingly popular sport. "Disc" has an official governing body, international championships and potential inclusion in future Olympic Games. It's time for Americans to break out the bandanas and start feeling the love for Ultimate Frisbee.

There was, admittedly, a time when Frisbee was not a legitimate sport. The first Wham-O Frisbees of the 1950s were, at the time, mere toys. Tossed at casual get-togethers and college campuses, Frisbees garnered little serious attention outside the canine community. This image has stuck. Many Americans view Frisbee as nothing more than a laid-back pastime—one primarily reserved for Starbucks baristas.

Behind the scenes, however, a Frisbee Renaissance had begun. In 1968, a group of New Jersey high schoolers invented Ultimate Frisbee, a sport combining the strategy of football, the athleticism of soccer, and the whirlwind pace of basketball with the unique loftiness of the Wham-O Frisbee. Two teams of seven (usually men and women) compete to connect passes for as many "touchdowns" as possible. Layouts, soaring grabs, exotic throws ("the scoober" is my personal favorite), and screaming hipsters only add to the appeal. Indeed, the game has grown by leaps and bounds. Between 2004 and 2011 alone, USA Ultimate (America's national Ultimate Frisbee organization) memberships grew from 10,000 to 16,000 players. "Disc" has also grown internationally, now played in forty-two countries worldwide. Frisbee is truly the ultimate new sport.

Why, then, is Disc dissed? The answer lies in the nature of the game itself. Ultimate—a self-consciously pure sport—has only one piece of equipment, no referees, no advertising agencies, no glittery stadiums, and no commercial interests to distract players from the joy of the game. It is a sport that relies on sportsmanship and integrity instead of jock attitude and fancy gear. This gives Ultimate Disc its hippie-anti-capitalist reputation, but also leaves the game unfortunately under-appreciated. No fancy gear means no big-money interest, so no media attention—thus Ultimate Frisbee flies under the radar of most Americans.

The ultimate question facing Disc enthusiasts is how to legitimize the game without corrupting it. Because corporate interest would undermine its counterculture core, Ultimate must rise to eminence through its players. Ultimate Frisbee is already soaring in popularity on college campuses and public parks across the globe. It is high time the American public caught on.

Sources

Avirgan, Jody. "Ultimate Frisbee at the Olympics?" The New York Times. The New York Times, 11 Aug. 2015. Web. 17 Mar. 2016.

Barta, Jasmine. "Ultimate Frisbee's Popularity Expands on Campuses." USA Today. Gannett, 03 June 2013. Web. 17 Mar. 2016.

Booth, Tina. "End the Marginalization of Ultimate in High Schools First." New York Times. 12 Aug. 2015. Web. 17 Mar. 2016.

"History of Ultimate." History of Ultimate. World Flying Disc Federation, n.d. Web. 17 Mar. 2016.

90 The N.H.L. Should Do Away With Fighting

by Adrian P. (2015)

In the 1970's, enforcers were a large part of N.H.L. teams' success. Rules were not strictly followed so these designated "tough guys" were signed on to teams to disincentivize dirty play from opposing players. The aggressive play of enforcers resulted in a slower-paced game, but teams would draw fewer penalties after an intervention by one of these physical skaters.

In the league today, fighting is an outdated practice. The rules have changed and improved to make player safety a priority. With strict rules and officiating and the implementation of video replay, teams no longer need a designated fighter to stop pests. With rule changes in the last ten to fifteen years there is simply no longer a need for players to risk head injury, their careers, and long term health by fighting on ice.

Hockey purists argue that enforcers still disincentivize dirty play in the N.H.L. "There is the argument that removing fighting would make the N.H.L. less safe, the notion that without the frozen frontier justice provided by enforcers, dirty players would take head shots and cheap shots with impunity." (Boston Globe) Referees also oversee fights, supposedly regulating and making them safer for players involved.

Statistics from the N.H.L. website have indicated that fights have been declining as teams have transitioned over to a more skilled game, as opposed to a physical style of play. Fighting has also been shown as detrimental to players' health, putting them at a higher risk for injuries, particularly to the head. Since 1980, teams in the top three for fighting have only finished at the top of the league ten times out of a possible 34.

The number of designated enforcers has declined as a result of a greater awareness of the risks of head trauma. The summer of 2011 hit the league hard with the news that three former enforcers had suffered from chronic traumatic encephalopathy and committed suicide, and another, Derek Boogaard, had been found to suffer from C.T.E. at age 28, in the prime of his career. Many people, former enforcers included, have since backed the elimination of fighting from hockey.

Fights no longer serve an important role in hockey today thanks to new technology, rule changes, and strict officiating. From the league's standpoint, trying to regulate fighting with a set of rules would lead to complex rulings. From a team's position, fights risk the health, both long and short term, of players. And from a player's perspective, a fight puts his health and career at risk and he may not even have helped his team for the act. The 'benefits' of an enforcer are now a non-factor and the NHL should do away with fighting.

Sources

Lehrer, Jonah. "Why We Travel." ScienceBlogs, 10 Dec. 2009. Web. 10 March 2014.

Branch, John. "Derek Boogaard: A Brain 'Going Bad.'" New York Times 5 Dec. 2011

Gasper, Christopher. "It's Time for NHL to End Fighting." Boston Globe 10 Feb. 2013: n. pag. Print.

91 "Chemical Horses" and the Racing Industry

by Erica Kirchhof (2015)

It was the day of Nehro's career-making race. He had trained months for this moment, running countless miles on unforgiving track in harrowing weather conditions. After all, placing second in the 2011 Kentucky Derby wasn't good enough for his trainers. Years of racing had withered Nehro's feet down to "little bitty nubs" with "bloody holes" (Drape). Nehro was at his breaking point. Finally, on the morning of the 2013 Kentucky Derby, Nehro painfully died of colic. He was five years old.

What kept Nehro on the track? The answer can be simplified to one word: drugs. Horse racing has turned into an inhumane money game where so many horses, like Nehro, are pumped with performance enhancing drugs just to win. Horse racing is a game, and the trainer with the cheapest horse and largest amount of earnings is the champion.

In March of last year PETA posted a video on their website that took the horse-racing world by storm. PETA's video centered around an undercover investigation that analyzed the daily racing routine of Steve Asmussen, a National Museum of Racing's Hall of Famer (Drape). The investigator reported Asmussen using drugs such as Lasix, thyroxine and phenylbutazone on horses for nontherapeutic purposes. Asmussen was allegedly racing horses that were chronically lame; some having rotting or bleeding hoofs (PETA investigation).

However, Asmussen is not the only trainer accused of horse abuse. Nineteen of the top 20 thoroughbred trainers in the United States have found on one account, to drug a horse before a race (Drape). These trainers are not at the top because of their horsemanship, but rather for their signature concoction of drugs injected into their top racing prospects.

Many people have argued that trainers and jockeys really care about the well-being of their horses. There have been many accounts of jockeys breaking down in tears when their mount had to be euthanized (Wilson).

While this may be true in some cases, the majority of trainers and jockeys care more about winning with drugs than the way their horse feels.

Horse racing has been an economical and cultural staple in the US for decades. By removing drugs from the horseracing industry, we can minimize track fatalities and weed out the industry's "cheaters." Let's modify racing to safer, more humane standards. It's time we started treating race horses like the athletes they really are.

Sources

Drape, Joe. "At Breeders' Cup, a Volatile Mix of Speed and Drugs." The New York Times, 03 Nov. 2010.

Drape, Joe. "PETA Accuses Two Trainers of Cruelty to Horses." The New York Times, 19 Mar. 2014.

"Horse Racing Exposed: Drugs and Death." PETA.org, 25 Feb. 2015.

Wilson, Art. "Why Not Focus on What's Good about the Sport?" Los Angeles Daily News, 14 Aug. 2014.

Criminal Justice and Policing

“At 12 years old, I learned about police brutality.”

“The sad reality for most victims of sexual violence is that their voice may never be heard or believed.”

“I have grown up in a town whose history and reputation centers around its two correctional facilities.”

92 Breaking the Blue Wall of Silence: Changing the Social Narrative About Policing in America

by Narain Dubey, 17 (2019)

As a child, I thought of police officers with veneration—if I saw a cop in the park, I felt safer. I told myself that when I got older, I would be wearing the badge too.

At 12 years old, I learned about police brutality. When I first saw the video of Eric Garner being thrown to the ground by police officers, I thought it was a movie. Despite knowing that the officers were at fault, I refused to change my internal rhetoric; I thought the media was only portraying the bad side of the people I saw as heroes.

Then on July 31, 2017, a police officer shot and killed my cousin, Isaiah Tucker, while he was driving. Isaiah wasn't just my cousin. He was also a young, unarmed, African-American man. I no longer dreamt of becoming a police officer.

But the issue is much larger than what happened to Isaiah. As highlighted in The New York Times, the Center for Policing Equity found that African-Americans are 3.6 times more likely to experience force by police officers as compared to whites.

Despite this blatant disproportionality, there is still overwhelming ignorance about it. Just last August, a group of people marched in Philadelphia, countering Black Lives Matter protests with signs and chants of "Blue Lives Matter." People are quick to challenge discussions of police violence with the idea that "not all cops are bad cops."

But when we argue in defense of the morality of individual police officers, we are undermining a protest of the larger issue: the unjust system of policing in the United States.

When I met Wesley Lowery, a journalist from The Washington Post, he was adamant that the social narrative regarding police brutality in the United States needs to change. "Conversations about police reform and accountability are about systems and structures, not about individuals," said Lowery.

It is not that some police officers aren't doing admirable things in our communities, but revering police officers for not abusing their power is dangerous—it normalizes police violence and numbs society to these issues. The idea that "not all cops are bad cops" belittles attempts to uproot the system. When we go out of our way to controvert this fight, we are perpetuating the inherent problems with racialized policing.

So as you think about policing in America, think of Eric Garner. Think of Alton Sterling, my cousin Isaiah, and the families that were left behind.

We have a responsibility as citizens of this country to call out corruption in systems of power. Policing in America is rooted in racism, oppression and privilege—it's time that we recognize that.

I learned to change my perspective. So can you.

Sources

Williams, Timothy. "Study Supports Suspicion That Police Are More Likely to Use Force on Blacks." New York Times. 7th July, 2016.

Lowery, Wesley. (2018, August 2nd). Personal communication at Asian American Journalist Association's JCAMP.

93 Rape: The Only Crime Where Victims Have to Explain Themselves

by Corinne Ahearn, 17 (2019)

"It's your choice if you want to press charges." The officer's eyes briefly met mine before he went back to shuffling papers. "But you won't win."

Instantly regretting getting the legal system involved, I knew the only thing that would come from this was my assaulter getting even more enraged.

The only way to describe the powerlessness I felt in that moment would be to compare it to the reason I was there in the first place.

The sad reality for most victims of sexual violence is that their voice may never be heard or believed.

"Rape is the only crime in which victims have to explain that they didn't want to be victimized," says Callie Rennison, a criminologist at the University of Colorado in Denver. As if survivors haven't gone through enough, they also deal with skepticism, victim-blaming, and rape myths. These are not only harmful to victims, but they skew the opinions of the general public on what rape really is.

You would never see a victim of a stabbing explaining that they didn't want to be stabbed. You would never see people claiming the victim lied about being stabbed for attention. Why isn't this the case for rape victims?

Victims are blamed less by the general public when the perpetrator was violently motivated rather than when the perpetrator was sexually motivated. Numerous studies have shown that victims of acquaintance rape were blamed more than victims of stranger rapes. The truth is, over 80% of all rape victims know their rapist personally, and rape doesn't have to be terrifyingly violent for it to still be rape. Just because a rape "could have been worse" doesn't excuse the fact that it's rape. Why do factors as small as these cause such a decrease in the validity of a survivor's story?

Not only do rape victims go through the initial trauma of the assault, but over 80% of survivors suffer from chronic physical or psychological conditions, the most common being post-traumatic stress disorder.

Thirty-three percent of women who are raped report contemplating suicide. Thirteen percent of women who are raped attempt suicide. These facts alone should hold enough weight to show that change is needed when it comes to the treatment of rape victims.

Fewer than 20 percent of all rapes and sexual assaults actually get reported to the police, a clear effect of these stereotypes and preconceived notions.

The statistics on those who bravely choose to press charges are all telling.

Of the small percentage of reported rapes, only eight percent are taken to trial.

In other words, 98.4 percent of rapists will get off without even going to trial.

That means only 0.006 percent of rapists are incarcerated.

Shocking? It should be.

Sources

Brody, Jane E. "The Twice-Victimized of Sexual Assault." The New York Times. 12 Dec. 2011.

Villines, Zawn. "Overcoming the Stigma of Sexual Assault: Know the Facts." Good Therapy, 26 June 2018.

Mitchell, Damon, et al. "Effects of Offender Motivation, Victim Gender, and Participant Gender on Perceptions of Rape Victims and Offenders." Journal of Interpersonal Violence, U.S. National Library of Medicine, Sept. 2009.

"Fast Facts: Sexual Assault." Bstigmafree.

94 Inmates Aren't Animals

by Marissa Brannick (2014)

I have grown up in a town whose history and reputation centers around its two correctional facilities: one maximum security, one super-maximum. For the majority of my life neither the prisons nor their inhabitants crossed my mind (even during the several school lock-downs due to escaped inmates, my main concern was the inconvenience), but recently I had the "pleasure" of visiting for the day.

Upon entering, my officer and tour guide referred to the inmates as "animals" and stated "act like an animal, and we treat you like an animal."

I began to question how effective this approach was considering the state of our nation's prison system, including rate of re-offense. It's time for America to try a new method: treat inmates with respect.

The New York Times editorial "Lessons From European Prisons" explored the fact that Europe has already been doing this for years. "Under German law, the primary goal of prison is 'to enable prisoners to lead a life of social responsibility free of crime upon release.' Public safety is ensured not simply by separating offenders from society, but by successfully reintegrating them." In German and Dutch prisons, inmates are able to live relatively normal lives focused on bettering themselves through rehabilitation, therapy, and education. Some are allowed to wear their own street clothes and prepare meals, living semi-independent lives. Therefore, when inmates are released from incarceration the change is not as drastic and they are ready to integrate into society instead of struggling to adapt to it.

In contrast, American offenders are punished by their country through voting-bans and roadblocks in finding jobs and housing. Inmates are forgotten as humans and remembered by their crimes. The book "The Other Wes Moore: One Name, Two Fates" by Wes Moore documents a man from boyhood to convict serving life and depicts the struggles one faces upon release; including the fact that prison can seem like a better alternative for those unable to assimilate to the outside world. Furthermore, it depicts low-income families and neighborhoods ruled by drugs and gangs that many incarcerated come from; they do not always have emotional, financial, or educational support and live in a world where partaking in illegal activities is their only viable future.

Upon imprisonment, these men and women are taken from this environment and welcomed by the same lack of support and faithless attitude. Society has failed these men and women and if we are to correct this we must ask what really came first: acting like an animal or being treated like one?

Sources

The Editorial Board. "Lessons From European Prisons." nytimes.com. The New York Times, 7 Nov. 2013. Web. 14 Mar. 2014. http://www.nytimes.com/2013/11/08/opinion/lessons-from-european-prisons.html.

Moore, Wes. The Other Wes Moore: One Name, Two Fates. New York: Spiegel & Grau, 2010. Print.

95 Life Sentences for Children Should Go Away . . . for Life

by Jessie Dietz, 17 (2019)

In 1993, Taurus Buchanan threw a single, deadly punch in a street fight among kids and was sentenced to life in prison without the possibility of parole. At the time of his arrest, Taurus, a young African American boy living in Louisiana, was a loving son, a hard worker, and a loyal friend. But most importantly, he was just a kid.

So why should Taurus, who was still a child at the time of his arrest, be given a sentence reserved for serial killers, cold-blooded murderers, and violent gang members? The answer is he shouldn't.

Life in prison for juveniles has been a phenomenon plaguing our nation for over 50 years. Even after the 2012 Supreme Court Case, Miller v. Alabama, which established that mandatory life sentences for children were unconstitutional, many children are still unjustly sentenced and forced to spend their formative years locked behind bars.

Currently, there are over 10,000 children incarcerated across America. Of those 10,000 children, 3,000 are serving life sentences without the possibility of parole. But prisons are dangerous places for children. While in prison, children are five times more likely to be sexually assaulted, are at an increased risk of suicide, and are exposed to violent and destructive behaviors.

A 2006 study, which tested juvenile offenders for the level of trauma they experienced while imprisoned, found that two-thirds of the incarcerated youths tested reported symptoms related to high aggression, depression, and anxiety. Even more shockingly, thirty percent reported a history of sexual or physical abuse, and eighty-four percent had tried marijuana at least once in their life.

So how can we solve this issue? The answer is placing a stronger emphasis on rehabilitation rather than punitive sentences for children. Research has shown that the human brain continues to develop through adolescence, with the prefrontal cortex, which is responsible for critical thinking and decision making, not fully developing until the mid-20's. This brain flexibility not only makes teenagers more susceptible to reckless behavior, but also makes them more amenable to rehabilitation than adults. In Missouri, one of the few states that places a strong emphasis on juvenile rehabilitation, only 8 percent of juvenile offenders who were rehabilitated were arrested again, representing its vast potential for success.

In almost every aspect of life, the U.S. acknowledges that children are unable to exercise the same kind of emotional and mental restraint as adults: they are unable to vote, serve on juries, or even drink. Regardless, when it comes to the criminal justice system, they are still subjected to the same repercussions as adults. We must continually challenge this egregious double standard, urging politicians to emphasize the importance of rehabilitation for juvenile offenders.

Sources

Armstrong, Ken, and Corey G. Johnson. "When He Was 16, This Man Threw One Punch—and Went to Jail for Life." Mother Jones, 4 Jan. 2016.

Cose, Ellis. "Rehabilitation Beats Punishment for Juveniles." Newsweek, 14 Jan. 2010.

Gottesman, David, and Susan Wile Schwarz. "Juvenile Justice in the U.S." National Center for Children in Poverty, July 2011.

Muller, Robert T. "Rehabilitation Benefits Young Offenders." Psychology Today, 17 Sept. 2015.

Robinson, Rashad. "No Child Deserves a Life Sentence. But Try Telling Prosecutors That." The New York Times, 10 Aug. 2017.

Roll Call Staff. "Youth Offenders Deserve a Chance for Rehabilitation." Roll Call, 11 Nov. 2009.

"United States: Thousands of Children Sentenced to Life without Parole." Human Rights Watch, 11 Oct. 2005.

96 It's Time to Legalize the World's Oldest Profession

by Ashlyn DesCarpentrie, 17 (2018)

Sex work is a legitimate occupation, and it's time we legalized it as such.

The truth is prostitution isn't going anywhere; it's called the "world's oldest profession" for a reason. Instead of squandering limited sources on policing an issue that history has proved impossible to eradicate, why not give sex work a legal framework that provides sex workers with medical help and legal protection against violence?

Prostitution is a multimillion dollar business, yet no one is collecting taxes from it.

According to Nevada brothel owner Dennis Hof, the city of Las Vegas alone could make $25 million a year, just from taxing prostitution. A study conducted by the University of California found that one American city spends on average of $2000 arresting one prostitute; this amounts to $125 million a year in enforcement costs nationwide.

Legalizing sex work would turn it into a revenue maker, rather than a burden for the taxpayer.

Making prostitution legal could minimize serious health concerns. Decriminalizing prostitution allows the government to regulate and monitor the trade. This, in turn, could ensure that HIV and other STD protection programs are carried out effectively, and research proves this to be true; according to expert Steffanie Strathdee's study, 46 percent of HIV infections could be averted in any of the Canadian, Kenyan and Indian cities she researched, simply by fully decriminalizing prostitution. An Australian study found that the prevalence of STDs was "80 times greater in 63 illegal street prostitutes than in 753 of their legal brothel counterparts". Additionally, it was found that condom use was significantly higher in legalized sex work compared to illegal prostitution.

It could be argued that authorizing sex work encourages ill treatment toward women. Research shows the opposite; legalizing prostitution actually reduces violence toward women. A study in the Netherlands found that opening designated legal street prostitution zones decreased rape and sexual abuse by 30-40 percent. It was also found that giving sex work a legal framework empowered women to demand safer sex and legal punishment of abuse. Furthermore, as Peter G. Hill brings up in his New York Times Letter to the Editor, legalizing prostitution allows the government to enforce age restrictions on sex trade, preventing underage teens from being lured into the trade.

I am not proclaiming a moral judgment on prostitution; I am stating facts. Prostitution is a reality of the modern world. This modern world demands equality. It demands protection and change. Yet change, protection and equality are not being demanded for sex workers. It's time for the government to stop telling people how to live their lives, and it's time for the citizens to demand protection for those who need it.

Sources

Akers, Mick. "This Pimp Wants to End Sex Trafficking." LasVegasSun.com, 20 March 2017.

Becklund, Laurie. "Prostitution Arrests Cost $2,000 Each, Study Finds." Los Angeles Times, Los Angeles Times, 10 July 1987.

Kastoryano, Stephen, et al. "Street Prostitution Zones and Crime." Cato Institute, 19 Apr. 2017.

"Opinion | Should Prostitution Be Legalized?" The New York Times, The New York Times, 7 Sept. 2015.

"Prostitution, Public Health, and Human-Rights Law." The Lancet.

"Simple Way to Curb HIV? Legalize Prostitution, AIDS Conference Told | CBC News." CBCnews, CBC/Radio Canada.

Consumer Culture

"When your favorite celebrity is wearing the newest jumper on the market and you just have to get your paws on a knock-off version, it can be hard to resist the urge to buy."

"The use of a poor, needy child in its image is a crucial aspect of the company's marketing."

"She was about to pour the seltzer into her girls' sippy cups when she noticed the fine print. The innocent-looking beverage contained 10 milligrams of CBD."

97 Shop Till You (And Humanity) Drop

by Emily Goldman, 16 (2016)

How many clothes do you actually wear in your closet? Did you ever stop to think where these clothes are going to go when they no longer fit your style? The desire of buying fast fashion may seem tempting, but the reality is as first world countries fill their closets with cheap trends, we continue to fill our landfills and our planet with harmful pollutants.

Every day consumers are bombarded with hypnotic advertisements, whether in a commercial or on social media. Social shopping is a main reason for wastefulness in the fashion industry because of how fast trends come and go. When your favorite celebrity is wearing the newest jumper on the market and you just have to get your paws on a knock-off version, it can be hard to resist the urge to buy. To add on, now it is easier than ever to purchase a quick impulse buy.

As of the first quarter of 2015, one third of online fashion purchases have been made on mobile devices. Kate Davidson Hudson, co-founder and chief executive of Editorialist states, "But now, everybody sees what's on the runways on social media and on blogs, and everybody's a critic, and shoppers want it as soon as they see it," she said. Americans need to be smarter about their purchases and recognize that every garment contributes to landfills for up to a staggering 80 years for that rubber soled shoe that was so last season.

Not only are clothes filling up our landfills, but the production process is also contributing to a series of unhealthy practices for our planet. Cotton alone consumes 10 percent of the world's agricultural chemicals and 25 percent of the world's pesticides. Annually, in the United States, the fashion industry contributes to around 25 billion pounds of textile waste, this is about 82 pounds per person.

Companies like Levi's and American Eagle have taken action into changing the way the clothing industry works by endorsing recycling campaigns.

These new contributions are helpful, but it is not enough. Americans need to become more consumer conscious and think before buying that cute get-up because sooner than later it will be in a landfill. I am not saying to stop shopping, I am saying that we should become aware of the chain reaction that our purchases contribute to, so we can become a less wasteful society as a whole.

Sources

"A Fast and Flat Fashion World." The New York Times.
"Gap's Fashion-Backward Moment." The New York Times.
"How Long Does It Take Garbage to Decompose?" About Money.
"Is the Fast Fashion Industry Ready to Change Its Wasteful Ways?" CBS News.

98 One-for-One Business Models: Do the Benefits of Philanthropic Companies Like Toms Outweigh the Harms?

by Lisa S., 15 (2016)

You've probably heard of them. You might even own a pair yourself. I, too, own a pair of Toms. For me, part of its initial appeal was the one-for-one slogan the company employs; for every pair sold, a pair is donated to children in need. Why not look good while doing good too? The shoes enable you to feel as though you're contributing positively to others without truly applying much effort.

The shoes might not actually "do good" after all. The company may be downright detrimental to the communities it claims to help. For one, Toms undermines local businesses, as they simply cannot compete with the free shoes. Studies have shown that large-scale foreign donations can have extremely harsh effects on local employment. A 2008 study found that clothing donations to Africa resulted in a 50 percent decline in the region's apparel employment.

Additionally, Laura Seay, a professor at Morehouse College, contends that by donating shoes, Toms is "just treating one symptom of a much deeper problem, and treating symptoms is not a cure." Poverty is the root cause of shoelessness. The people who receive footwear do have access to cheap shoes but not the money to purchase them, and Toms is not doing much to address this problem at all. The business itself actually needs impoverished children to thrive. The use of a poor, needy child in its image is a crucial aspect of the company's marketing.

The shoes are not sturdy either. They last three months on average, but this time can be stretched to seven or eight months if cared for properly. Shoe drops occur about every two years; this, in conjunction with the very limited life expectancy of the shoes, is clearly not enough to sustain the children, especially those who live in rockier regions.

Toms has made steps in the right direction. It has launched an eyewear line that contributes to an increase in medical employees who provide support for people in need of improved vision. This allows them to become employable and break the cycle of poverty. Additionally, Toms has begun to manufacture shoes locally in places such as Haiti and Ethiopia, which opens up job opportunities for people living in the area. Due to the small numbers of people they benefit, these decisions don't solve everything. However, they begin to address some of the criticism Toms has received over the years.

A pair of Toms is expensive, costing a hefty 55 dollars for canvas slip-ons. Overall, despite Toms' efforts, these 50 plus dollars would be much better off being donated to a charity that can work to make actual progress concerning poverty, in areas such as infrastructure, education or health.

Sources

Chu, Jeff. "Toms Sets Out to Sell a Lifestyle, Not Just Shoes." Fast Company. 17 Jun. 2013.

Downtown Miami and Brickell: Chamber of Commerce. "Haiti to Begin Manufacturing Toms Shoes." Miami Herald. 29 Sept. 2013.

Herrera, Adriana. "Questioning the Toms Model for Social Enterprise." The New York Times. 19 Mar. 2013.

Otto, Isaac. "Toms Shoes Responds to Critics, but It May Not Be Enough." Mercy Corps. 24 Jul. 2013.

99 Why Mainstreaming CBD In Consumer Products Is Detrimental To Our Society

by Emily Milgrim, 15 (2019)

One recent morning, my aunt's family went to a local bakery. Her toddler-aged daughters love seltzer, and a pink pastel can, labeled "Recess," on display caught their eyes. My aunt thought they were adorable—what could be wrong with a pastel can with a playful name? She was about to pour the seltzer into her girls' sippy cups when she noticed the fine print. The innocent-looking beverage contained 10 milligrams of CBD.

It's preposterous that there is no requirement to include a warning, and that the store is not required, at a minimum, to alert the purchaser of the ingredient. Many CBD products have no age restrictions. Because my aunt was educated on the subject, she saved her children from potential harm. However, many uneducated consumers are unaware they are consuming cannabinoids, or their potential effects.

So, what's the big deal with CBD? Why is it being marketed in everyday items?

CBD, also known as Cannabidiol, is highly commercialized as an additive in simple pleasures from ice cream to dog treats. CBD is a chemical compound found in the Cannabis plant that does not cause the 'stoned' effect that is associated with its sister compound, tetrahydrocannabinol (THC). This makes hemp-derived CBD currently legal in all 50 states. It is marketed to cure pains and anxiety, and is being experimented with medically. CBD may also have adverse effects such as anxiety, diarrhea, dizziness, and vomiting, just to name a few.

Many consumers believe that the benefits of CBD outweigh the possible side effects. However, this is not the case. Exposing an unneeded, drug-like substance to audiences who don't medically require it opens gates to experimentation with its sister, THC. Having Cannabidiol marketed towards younger crowds, including items that attract very young children, such as desserts or soda, kickstarts this exposure to our society prematurely. Joe Camel cannot sell cigarettes anymore, so why is a pink soda can named "Recess" with CBD allowed?

According to the Journal of the American Medical Association, in 2017, nearly 70 percent of all CBD products sold online were incorrectly labeled, and in some cases may have included other compounds such as THC. Moreover, the adverse effects of CBD are being studied in pregnant and nursing mothers, including developmental defects and the increased permeability of the placental barrier. Luckily, my aunt, a nursing mother, noticed this ingredient before consumption.

With these potential ramifications, should CBD be marketed towards shoppers in a non-medical environment? Absolutely not. All items containing CBD should require 21-plus identification when purchased, and warning labels should be mandated to alert consumers of possible effects. We must push for stricter legislation to regulate the non-medical marketing of CBD.

Sources

"America's CBD Boom: Brazen Claims, Fake Products, Regulatory Scrutiny." The Business of Fashion, 17 Feb. 2019.

Chaker, Anne Marie. "Cannabis Comes to Your Coffee and Candy—but Is it Legal?" The Wall Street Journal, 12 Sept. 2018.

Williams, Alex. "Why Is CBD Everywhere?" The New York Times, 27 Oct. 2018.

Wong, Cathy. "CBD Oil: Benefits, Uses, Side Effects and Safety." Verywell Health, 6 Mar. 2019.

100 "Cultural Appropriation" Is Critical to Human Progress

by Maggie Strauss, 17 (2019)

A skirt on Zara. A Dior campaign. Keziah Daum's prom dress. What do all of these things have in common? They are the latest victims of America's politically correct crusaders.

In today's "cancel" culture, people are quick to attack others for behaving in a way they deem socially unacceptable. Central to many of these accusations is the idea of cultural appropriation: the adoption of the customs, practices, or ideas of one society by a member of another.

The fashion industry in particular has come under severe scrutiny in the past year for "stealing" traditions. As Vanessa Friedman writes in "Fashion's Year in Cultural Don'ts", the aforementioned skirt was too similar to an Indian lungi, the Dior campaign drew too much inspiration from the Mexican escaramuzas, and Keziah Daum's qipao was too Asian for her.

These fashion statements were clearly not designed to offend or degrade the cultures that influenced them. However, that is not to say that everyone who draws inspiration from different cultures is doing it with the right intentions. Issues arise when imitation is based on a shallow and offensive stereotype, which is just blatant racism.

Cultural appropriation is not a modern concept; it has existed as long as culture itself. From a historical perspective, the term that is typically used to describe the adoption of certain practices from one culture to the next is syncretism. Without syncretism, human progress would be next to impossible.

Often referred to throughout history as a "melting pot," America is a perfect example of the importance of syncretism. Immigrants from diverse backgrounds can all come together under a common American nationality. Pizza, hot dogs, and soft drinks are often considered characteristically American, but they were originally Italian, German, and Swedish, respectively. Is this cultural appropriation? Even Democracy, the very basis of American society, was first seen in ancient Greece. Is it time to "cancel" America?

Obviously not. But what makes drinking a carbonated beverage so different from wearing a Chinese-inspired prom dress? Cultural appropriation is just the modern term for a concept that has aided in the development of human society for centuries. Those who perpetuate "cancel" culture ignore this. And that has dangerous implications for the future.

Limiting oneself to dressing and acting as one's heritage determines is dangerously close to a "separate but equal" mentality. As George Chesterton writes for GQ, "If we can only exist in and guard the cultures we emerged from, from those we resemble, we will shrink into the superficiality of newly contrived tribes." Without embracing and building upon the ideas of other cultures, humanity remains static. History has proven that "cultural appropriation" is critical for human progress, and without it the future is bleak.

Sources

Chesterton, George. "Cultural Appropriation: Everything Is Culture and It's All Appropriated." GQ, 15 Jan. 2019.

Friedman, Vanessa. "Fashion's Year in Cultural Don'ts." The New York Times, 21 Dec. 2018.

APPENDIX A

The Rubric and Rules for the NYTLN Student Editorial Contest

RUBRIC AND RULES FOR THE NEW YORK TIMES LEARNING NETWORK ANNUAL STUDENT EDITORIAL CONTEST

Rules:

1. You can write your editorial about any topic you like, as long as you use at least one source from The Times.
2. Use at least one non-Times source. But make sure that the source you use is a reliable one. We encourage you to find sources that offer different perspectives on an issue.
3. Always cite your sources. Our submission form contains a required field for entering your citations. We include an example as well, though you can use M.L.A. or A.P.A. styles, or just list the web addresses. Even if you use a print source or an expert interview, you must provide a citation. Readers (and judges) should always be able to tell where you got your evidence. However, there is no need to provide in-text citations.
4. The editorial must not exceed 450 words. Your title and list of sources are separate, however, and do not count as part of your 450-word limit.
5. Have an opinion. Editorials are different from news articles because they try to persuade readers to share your point of view. Don't be afraid to take a stand.

6. Write your editorial by yourself or with a group, but please submit only one editorial per student. If you are working as a team, just remember to submit all of your names when you post your entry. And if you're submitting as part of a team, you should not also submit as an individual.
7. Be original and use appropriate language. Write for a well-informed audience, but include enough background information to give context. Be careful not to plagiarize. Use quotation marks around lines you take verbatim from another source, or rephrase and cite your source.
8. We will use the rubric below to judge entries, and the winning editorials will be featured on The Learning Network. Your work will be judged by Times journalists, Learning Network staff members and educators from around the country.

THE NEW YORK TIMES LEARNING NETWORK STUDENT EDITORIAL CONTEST RUBRIC

	Excellent (4)	Proficient (3)	Developing (2)	Beginning (1)
Viewpoint: Editorial states a clear opinion and issues a call to action through argument based on evidence.				
Evidence: Editorial uses compelling evidence to support the opinion, and cites reliable sources.				
Analysis and Persuasion: Editorial convincingly argues point of view by providing relevant background information, using valid examples, acknowledging counter-claims, and developing claims—all in a clear and organized fashion.				
Language: Editorial has a strong voice and engages the reader. It uses language, style and tone appropriate to its purpose and features correct grammar, spelling and punctuation.				
Guidelines: Editorial follows all contest guidelines, including the citation of at least one Times and one non-Times source				

APPENDIX B

Covid-19 and the Teen Response: Three Essays from Our Spring 2020 Contest

The 2020 Learning Network Editorial Contest was open to submission from February 13 to April 21, well after this book had moved into production. The contest began just as the first cases of coronavirus in the U.S. were detected, ran through the weeks when schools across the nation moved online, and ended just before some states began to "reopen." Though teenagers from Asia and Europe submitted essays on the pandemic throughout, the first wave of essays from American students barely mentioned the coronavirus. Those that came in toward the end of the submission period, however, were consumed with it.

Given how profoundly this crisis has impacted every aspect of teenage life, perhaps it is not surprising that there turned out to be nearly as many ways to write about Covid-19 as there were students writing about it. For many, it added urgency to the social justice issues that already mattered to them, and they wrote passionately through a Covid-19 lens about racism and xenophobia, income inequality, prison reform, hunger, homelessness, voting rights, the digital divide, climate change, and more.

For others, it presented new questions to think about, from the rights of frontline workers to the problem of toilet-paper hoarding. Some focused on the politics of the pandemic, but many more found a way to make the personal universal. These essayists honed larger arguments out of their individual experiences of loneliness and anxiety; their disappointment in missing proms and graduations; their changing relationships with parents, siblings, friends, and teachers; and the books, movies, music, and video games that kept them occupied for weeks in quarantine.

Though we hadn't finished judging the contest when this book went to press, we felt the teenage response to the crisis deserved an addendum. Here are three excellent essays from 2020 that are representative of the submissions overall. All three exhibit the kinds of sophisticated "writer's moves" recommended in the Teacher's Companion to this book, from "connect personal experience to a larger point" to "make your conclusions memorable." But together they also show that it's possible to take something impacting nearly every human on earth and, nonetheless, make it your own.

Three Essays on Covid-19

101 This Land Was Made for You and Me

by Nicole Tian, 15

"Welcome home!" The US customs agent smiles at me, handing me my deep blue passport embossed with a golden eagle. America is my home, where I can celebrate Lunar New Year and drive up to San Francisco five months later to cheer with strangers, united under fireworks on the Fourth of July.

Picture an American on Independence Day. Picture a Chinese. Now, picture a girl, a product of these two cultures, smiling so wide her cheeks hurt as the night rumbles awake. The dark hides her face and skin-tone. Her silhouette against the sky outlines the features of a patriot.

Now, the novel SARS-CoV-2 virus has transformed part of my identity into a slur. My own president designated the pandemic as the "Chinese Virus," a moniker that implicates a whole culture and its descendants, inviting fear and offering up Asian Americans as easy targets.

Inflammatory languages lead to violent actions. Reports of bigotry against Asian Americans recently spiked. Clearly, this violence is misguided. The viruses are blind to ethnicity. Not every Chinese American has COVID-19, and not everyone who has tested positive is of Chinese descent.

To confront the coronavirus and alienation, the Chinese American community has gone to great lengths to mobilize in slowing the virus's spread. However, my community's good will is misunderstood by some as a plea to be accepted as American, a submissive gesture from the "model minority" to please the system that is constructed against us. Indeed, prominent members like former Democratic presidential candidate Andrew Yang have called upon Chinese-Americans to increase their efforts at patriotism to escape stigma. According to his argument, Asian Americans must volunteer vigorously, wave the flag more enthusiastically and spin their tale into one of diehard patriotism to prove their rights for being in this country.

Novelist Toni Morrison pointed out the truth of this strained effort to prove one's Americanness, commenting "in this country American means white. Everybody else has to hyphenate." Yang reinforces the idea that hyphenation means not fully American, not fully loyal, and connotes a degree of separation from being American.

The peril of social division is not just about our president and politicians' literacy and decency, but of ours. As citizens of this country, we, born here or naturalized, are obligated to join the collective effort to stop the virus. It is also our responsibility to call out another form of pathogens in our systems and structures. The use of "Chinese virus" is rooted in ethnocentrism and racism, which not only undermines our civility but also comes at a cost to human lives.

You and I are both Americans, featured differently, but committed equally to the well-being of our country.

Picture Americans, you and me.

Sources

Goodreads. www.goodreads.com/quotes/157837-in-this-country-american-means-white-everybody-else-has-to. Accessed 20 Apr. 2020.

Tavernise, Sabrina, and Richard A. Oppel, Jr. "Spit On, Yelled At, Attacked: Chinese-Americans Fear for Their Safety." The New York Times, 23 Mar. 2020. The New York Times, www.nytimes.com/2020/03/23/us/chinese-coronavirus-racist-attacks.html?searchResultPosition=1. Accessed 20 Apr. 2020.

Yang, Andrew. "We Asian Americans are not the virus, but we can be part of the cure." The Washington Post, 1 Apr. 2020. The Washington Post, www.washingtonpost.com/opinions/2020/04/01/andrew-yang-coronavirus-discrimination/?tid=lk_inline_manual_21&itid=lk_inline_manual_21. Accessed 20 Apr. 2020.

102 The Eagle of Freedom: Birdcage Edition

by Nicholas Parker, 17

From fringe Facebook groups inciting rebellion against their state's quarantine precautions to our basic inability to stop touching our faces, Americans really hate to follow rules. If we, as a country, are going to survive the global pandemic of COVID-19, we're going to have to suppress some of the national character traits that make us who we are.

The American personality is brash, bold, and in love with its privileges, liberties and freedoms. We formed our country through rebellion against an authoritarian regime. Our heroes recast paradigms and break rules. Our national character resists our attempt to cage our pursuit of happiness.

A Pew Research Center poll in mid-April found that 51 percent of Republicans and Republican leaners were worried the country will reopen too quickly for safety, while 48 percent feared it wouldn't happen quickly enough. Even within a single political party, that's a spread of opinion as diverse as the American psyche and just as conflicted.

As federal, state and local governments struggle to find a balance between their citizens' safety and right to make their own decisions, demonstrators have gathered to campaign for the end of quarantine. What we need to do to survive is adhere to caution and common sense, which is hard to do when our national leadership recklessly panders to fringe groups for political gain. As protesters prepared to rally in states with Democratic governors, President Trump egged them on with tweets of "LIBERATE..."

Protest signs included legends such as "Let my people GO-LF" and "Social distancing = Communism."

Even simple admonitions by health officials to stop touching one's face provoke a complex compulsion to do that very thing. In the age of the COVID-19 pandemic, it's verboten to risk putting germs and viruses near one's orifices, but we just can't stop the feeling.

If we can't tame these urges, will marketers be reduced to serving up public service announcements on the hazards of hairline handling? Will works of art featuring personal probing be prohibited like cigarette advertising? Will finger foods become forbidden fruit?

It is a dark, dystopian world where even for a short time citizens must cultivate their own coiffures, miss a massage and feed with family. It's obvious this quarantine will have drastic consequences for the economy and the families that make up that economy. However, there will be catastrophic consequences if we can't curb the part of our national identity that insists on getting what we want when we want it. We need to set aside our fears that this is the end of the world today and have enough common sense that it doesn't become the end of the world tomorrow.

Sources

Russonello, Giovanni. "What's Driving the Right-Wing Protestors Fighting the Quarantine?" The New York Times, 17 Apr. 2020.

"Most Americans Say Trump Was Too Slow in Initial Response to Coronavirus Threat." Pew Research Center for the People and the Press. Pew Research Center, 16 Apr. 2020.

Parker-Pope, Tara. "Stop Touching Your Face!" The New York Times, 2 Mar. 2020.

Casiano, Louis. "Republicans Bash Facebook for Stopping Promotion of Protests that Would Defy Social-Distancing Guidelines." Fox News, 20 Apr. 2020.

103 How Animal Crossing Will Save Gen Z

by Ananya Udaygiri, age 15

Generation Z was born in the aftermath of 9/11, molded by the economic recession of 2008, and polished off by the coronavirus, the worst pandemic in a century. And that doesn't even include the mounting crisis of climate change. Or the growing nationalism. Or the gun violence epidemic. Gen Z's childhood is rooted in issues that would be unrecognizable only a decade prior. We are no strangers to a fight. So what drew us to a Japanese video game about living in a village with anthropomorphic animal neighbors? Like moths to a flame, or, perhaps more appropriately, like children to their first love, Animal Crossing has captured the young teenage heart.

Animal Crossing is a video game made by Nintendo in the early 2000s. The game's iterations and evolutions have mirrored our developments throughout grade school, and now, when the curtains of our childhood begin to close, Animal Crossing's masterpiece has taken the stage. Animal Crossing: New Horizons, the latest version of the game, is now a staple of Generation Z's culture. The characters in the game connected with my generation at a level never seen before. Yet in Animal Crossing, the characters live virtually unrecognizable lives.

The basic premise of Animal Crossing is small-town living. Your character, a human villager, performs basic, everyday functions. You fish. You catch bugs. You grow a tree. Common themes are relaxation and simplicity. Even the soundtrack is purposely designed as a calm lullaby, which harks back to simpler times today's teens have only dreamed of. It's a stark contrast to the chaos of our lives. In a New York Times article focusing on Animal Crossing in the age of coronavirus, the author described how Animal Crossing was a "miniature escape" for those isolated by the pandemic. He labeled it a "balm" for the "rushing tonnage of real-world news." While that is certainly true, for Generation Z it encompasses all that and more.

The characters in the game don't have to worry about school shootings, arbitrary college admissions, or the rapidly deteriorating environment. They simply... live. For a generation that has been denied safety, a voice, and now, as the final blow, the coming-of-age traditions of prom and graduation, Animal Crossing represents a Gen Z vision for better times.

There are those who seek to diminish my generation's concerns. They cite the suffering of others and admonish us for our presumptuousness. But sadness is never relative to others. Our generation's troubles are valid and growing. Buzzfeed News so aptly describes it as a "generation free fall." So pick up your video game console. Load in Animal Crossing. Play the game. For Generation Z, Animal Crossing is hope, and it will save us all.

Sources

Brodeur, Michael Andor. "The Animal Crossing Soundtrack Is an Unlikely Lullaby for a Nervous World." The Washington Post, 21 Apr. 2020.

Brooks, Ryan. "The Coronavirus Pandemic Has Put Gen Z And Young Millennials' Lives On Hold." 20 Apr. 2020.

Buchanan, Kyle. "Animal Crossing Is the Perfect Way to Spend Quarantine." New York Times, 31 Mar. 2020.

About the Author

Katherine Schulten was editor-in-chief of The New York Times Learning Network from 2006 to 2019 and is still a contributing editor there. She grew up in Texas and began her career in education right after college, when she served as a Jesuit Volunteer with middle school students in Brooklyn, New York. From there, she briefly taught in Japan, then spent 10 years as an English teacher at Brooklyn's Edward R. Murrow High School, where she was also advisor to the school newspaper.

After winning a Prudential Fellowship to the Columbia School of Journalism, Katherine worked for nine years in schools all over the city as a literacy consultant for the New York City Writing Project. In that role she focused on Career and Technical Education, helping teachers infuse writing into subjects across the curriculum, from science and math to plumbing and cosmetology.

Katherine is also on the board of Literacy for Incarcerated Teens, a non profit which gets books and writing programs into New York state detention facilities for young people. She lives in Brooklyn with her husband and is the mother of twins now in their twenties.

accountability are about systems and structures, not about individuals," said Lowery.

It is not that some police officers aren't doing admirable things in our communities, but revering police officers for not abusing their power is dangerous—it normalizes police violence and numbs society to these issues. The idea that "not all cops are bad cops" belittles attempts to uproot the system. When we go out of our way to controvert this fight, we are perpetuating the inherent problems with racialized policing.

So as you think about policing in America, think of Eric Garner. Think of Alton Sterling, my cousin Isaiah, and the families that were left behind.

We have a responsibility as citizens of this country to call out corruption in systems of power. Policing in America is rooted in racism, oppression and privilege—it's time that we recognize that.

I learned to change my perspective. So can you.

Sources

Williams, Timothy. "Study Supports Suspicion That Police Are More Likely to Use Force on Blacks." New York Times. 7th July, 2016.

Lowery, Wesley. (2018, August 2nd). Personal communication at Asian American Journalist Association's JCAMP.

93 Rape: The Only Crime Where Victims Have to Explain Themselves

by Corinne Ahearn, 17 (2019)

"It's your choice if you want to press charges." The officer's eyes briefly met mine before he went back to shuffling papers. "But you won't win."

Instantly regretting getting the legal system involved, I knew the only thing that would come from this was my assaulter getting even more enraged.

The only way to describe the powerlessness I felt in that moment would be to compare it to the reason I was there in the first place.

The sad reality for most victims of sexual violence is that their voice may never be heard or believed.

"Rape is the only crime in which victims have to explain that they didn't want to be victimized," says Callie Rennison, a criminologist at the University of Colorado in Denver. As if survivors haven't gone through enough, they also deal with skepticism, victim-blaming, and rape myths. These are not only harmful to victims, but they skew the opinions of the general public on what rape really is.

You would never see a victim of a stabbing explaining that they didn't want to be stabbed. You would never see people claiming the victim lied about being stabbed for attention. Why isn't this the case for rape victims?

Victims are blamed less by the general public when the perpetrator was violently motivated rather than when the perpetrator was sexually motivated. Numerous studies have shown that victims of acquaintance rape were blamed more than victims of stranger rapes. The truth is, over 80% of all rape victims know their rapist personally, and rape doesn't have to be terrifyingly violent for it to still be rape. Just because a rape "could have been worse" doesn't excuse the fact that it's rape. Why do factors as small as these cause such a decrease in the validity of a survivor's story?

Not only do rape victims go through the initial trauma of the assault,